Democracy and Deliberation

Democracy and Deliberation

New Directions for Democratic Reform

James S. Fishkin

Yale University Press

New Haven and London

Designed by Sonia L. Scanlon
Set in Trump type by The Composing
Room of Michigan, Inc.
Printed in the United States of America by
Vail-Ballou Press, Binghamton, New York.

Library of Congress Cataloging-in-Publication Data

Fishkin, James S.
    Democracy and deliberation : new directions
for democratic reform / James S. Fishkin.
        p.   cm.
    Includes bibliographical references and index.
    ISBN 0-300-05161-1 (cloth)
             0-300-05163-8 (pbk.)
    1. Democracy.   I. Title.
JC423.F63   1991
321.8—dc20   91-24929
                                                   CIP

A catalogue record for this book is available from
the British Library.

The paper in this book meets the guidelines for
permanence and durability of the Committee on
Production Guidelines for Book Longevity of the
Council on Library Resources.

10 9 8 7 6 5 4 3 2

Contents

Acknowledgments

This book had its origins in an idea that I conceived as a fellow at the Center for Advanced Study in the Behavioral Sciences at Stanford during the academic year 1987–88. Many of the fellows and staff of the center helped me, particularly Gordon Wood, Larry Bartels, Bob Scott, John Kingdon, and Nan and Bob Keohane. I would also like to thank Jack Beatty, who facilitated the original publication of the idea in the *Atlantic*.

Our effort to demonstrate practical variants of the idea had its origins with Max and Jeffrey Kampelman. Max had the initial insight to suggest working with WETA, the Washington PBS affiliate, and Jeffrey became my partner in attempting to develop a demonstration of the idea. I am also very grateful to our colleagues on the project at WETA, particularly Dick Richter, Richard Hutton, and Ed Fouhy. Betty Sue Flowers offered crucial help. At various stages, Ward Chamberlain and Sharon Rockefeller were indispensable in recognizing the value of the idea and in determining that it deserved to be realized.

I believe that the genesis for this project was greatly influenced by certain teachers and/or former colleagues of mine at Yale, particularly Robert Dahl, Bruce Ackerman, Ed Lindblom, and Doug Rae. Giovanni Sartori and Peter Laslett also gave me wonderful advice and encouragement. Walter Dean Burnham gave me crucial help on every part of the manuscript. Jeff Tulis, Calvin Johnson, Bruce Buchanan, Rudy de la Garza, Robert Luskin, Sandy Levinson, Bob King, and Scott Powe provided valuable advice on various sections. I would like to thank Paul Woodruff and Michael Gagarin for discussions on ancient Greek democracy. On issues of sampling and methodology, Mel Hinich was indispensable. On the comparative side, I have benefited from the help of Philippe Schmitter, Claus Offe, and, most especially, Archie Brown. I am also grateful to David Braybrooke, Tom Seung, and Cass Sunstein for enriching the democratic

theory sections. Bill Galston gave me crucial advice, both theoretical and practical.

The central portions of this manuscript were presented at a
conference sponsored by the Center for the Study of Democracy
in Sofia, Bulgaria, in December 1990 and at a conference sponsored by UNAM and CIDE in Mexico City in January 1991. On
both occasions I benefited greatly from comments of the participants.

In closing, I want to thank Tina Weiner of Yale University
Press for the initial suggestion that my *Atlantic* article could
become the impetus for a short book. Most especially, I want to
thank my wife, Shelley, and my father-in-law, Milton Fisher, for
their continuing encouragement and insight at every stage.
They energized the entire family to bring this project to fruition.

Part One
Introduction

Toward a New Democracy

This book is about how to bring power to the people under conditions where the people can think about the power they exercise. It is, in short, about how to reconcile democracy and deliberation.

It is part of a 2,500-year quest to better adapt the democratic idea, originally suited to populations of several thousand in a Greek city-state, to populations of many millions in a modern megastate. It is about how we might bring some of the favorable characteristics of small-group, face-to-face democracy to the large-scale nation-state. This quest will take us through a broad range of historical and theoretical topics, including the debates of the American Founders, the use of juries selected by lot in Athenian democracy, the transformations in the American system of presidential selection, the attempted transitions to democracy in Eastern Europe, and the rationale behind a new kind of democratic event that can be used to launch the next season of presidential selection.

This book will focus on possible solutions as much as on seemingly insoluble problems. It will put forward the notion of a "deliberative opinion poll" as a mechanism for combining political equality with deliberation. An ordinary opinion poll models what the public thinks, given how little it knows. A deliberative opinion poll models what the public *would* think, if it had a more adequate chance to think about the questions at issue.[1] Among other uses, deliberative opinion polls offer a way out of the dilemma which, as we will see, has afflicted American efforts to bring greater democracy to presidential selection. On the one hand, the proliferation of mass primaries has largely emptied the process of deliberation. On the other hand, a return to the smoked-filled rooms that once dominated candidate selection would sacrifice political equality. We seem to face a forced choice between politically

equal but relatively incompetent masses and politically unequal but relatively more competent elites.

Institutions designed on the model of the deliberative opinion poll escape this dilemma. They embody political equality
because everyone has an equal chance of being represented in
the national sample of participants. But they also embody deliberation because they immerse a selected group of citizens in
intensive, face-to-face debate.

Imagine a new beginning to the process of selecting a president. A crucial fact about the American process of candidate
selection is that it is extremely "front-loaded": that is, early
results greatly influence those which follow. Hence, a different
process at the outset could have a dramatic effect on the eventual results. In this new beginning, a national sample of the
citizen voting-age population is transported to a single site for at
least several days.[2] These "delegates" are given the opportunity
to interact in person with the major candidates of each party.
Democratic delegates go to the Democratic events, Republicans
to the Republican events; independents are asked beforehand to
choose one or the other. In some portions of the event, the entire
convention meets together. Some of the candidate appearances
before these groups are individual, while some are in debate
formats. Many of these occasions for questioning and interaction are broadcast on national television. After debating the
issues with the candidates and with each other, the delegates are
polled on their preferences on both the candidates and the issues.

If this event were formally institutionalized, it would
amount to what I have called a "National Caucus."[3] It would be
charged with selecting a certain number of at-large delegates to
the national conventions of the two major parties. The number
of delegates need not be large. The number selected in Iowa or
New Hampshire, for example, is quite small. Those two states
have an extraordinary impact on the selection process because
of the timing of their events and the ensuing media attention,
not because of the number of delegates selected.

As of this writing, plans are at an advanced stage for an unofficial version of this basic experiment in the 1992 presidential cycle. The Public Broadcasting Service (PBS) has scheduled a "National Issues Convention," organized on the deliberative opinion poll model, to be broadcast on national television over the weekend of January 17–19, 1992. The program will be produced by WETA, the Washington, D.C., PBS affiliate. The scheduled site for the event is the campus of the University of Texas at Austin. The candidates will interact with a national sample of six hundred delegates representing the entire electorate. These delegates will discuss the issues with the candidates over a three-day period and express their preferences on both the issues and the candidates.[4] At this writing, full funding for the event has not yet been secured, but the serious effort under way shows how the viability of the idea can be demonstrated without legislation or any formal change in the presidential selection process.[5]

The distinctive promise of this innovation is best seen against the history of recent efforts to reform, and to reform the reforms in, the presidential nominating system. The system that nominated Hubert Humphrey and Richard Nixon in 1968 has been massively democratized and popularized since then. It has been made more dependent on primaries and on timely participation by the rank and file. Although the proliferation of primaries ensures that the system will never return to its former state, the pendulum has swung partway back. Affirmative action for party elites, awarding them spots as "super delegates," assures them more influence on the process than they had when Jimmy Carter was first nominated in 1976. But whatever the degree of counter-reform, the changes back and forth have moved within too narrow a range of options, too narrow a vision of democratic possibilities. Our tinkering with the system has been constricted by a false dilemma: that we must choose between the thoughtful but antidemocratic competence of elites on the one hand, and the superficialities of mass democracy on the other. Either we have smoke-filled rooms or we end up choosing our candidates more or less the way we choose detergents.

Deliberative opinion polls offer a new kind of democracy, one that combines deliberation and political equality. Ordinarily, the electorate has very spotty information and limited occasions for thoughtful interaction on public issues. A deliberative opinion poll gives to a microcosm of the entire nation the opportunities for thoughtful interaction and opinion formation that are normally restricted to small-group democracy. It brings the face-to-face democracy of the Athenian Assembly or the New England town meeting to the large-scale nation-state. Most important, it offers a face-to-face democracy not of elected members of a legislature, but of ordinary citizens who can participate on the same basis of political equality as that offered by the assembly or town meeting.[6] It provides a statistical model of what the electorate *would* think if, hypothetically, all voters had the same opportunities that are offered to the sample in the deliberative opinion poll.[7]

The ultimate point of such a poll is prescriptive, not predictive. Its results have prescriptive force because they are the voice of the people under special conditions where the people have had a chance to think about the issues and hence should have a voice worth listening to.

It has long been known that ordinary opinion polls have a major effect on campaigns. They are an important part of what has come to be called the "invisible primary," the jockeying for visibility and credibility in the media that precedes the Iowa caucuses and the New Hampshire primary, the first events of the official primary season.[8] Similarly, it should be possible for a deliberative opinion poll to play a major role in the invisible primary. Instead of measuring the unreflective preferences of mass citizens, it would measure the refined public opinion that would result from more thoughtful interactions.

Such an event offers a means of launching candidacies and issues in a competition that is more representative of the entire country than either Iowa or New Hampshire and more deliberative than our conventional campaign process. With a deliberative opinion poll positioned as the first event, the rest of the primary season can proceed as before. This proposal is not intended to replace the race for the presidency as we know it; rather, it is intended to alter the way the race is started.

The presidential selection system, as it has been progressively democratized, is governed to a large extent by momentum. Early victories and defeats have an enormous effect on later primaries and caucuses.[9] Morris Udall, a Democratic candidate in 1976, described the impact of Jimmy Carter's early successes as being "like a football game in which you say to the first team that makes a first down with ten yards, 'Hereafter your team has a special rule. Your first downs are five yards. And if you make three of those you get a two-yard first down. And we're going to let your first touchdown count twenty-one points. Now the rest of you bastards play catch-up under the regular rules.'"[10]

While some have interpreted the 1988 elections as undermining the role of momentum, there is in fact strong evidence to the contrary. The argument that momentum was less of a factor than in previous elections turns on the eventual fates of Richard Gephardt and Bob Dole, the Democratic and Republican winners in Iowa in 1988. But Robert Lichter notes that both Gephardt and Dole were far behind the New Hampshire front-runners on January 30 (before the Iowa results). "After their Iowa victories, each closed the gap by 14 percentage points—not a bad little hop," he concludes. "Unfortunately that left Gephardt still nineteen points behind Dukakis, and it left Dole eight points behind Bush. . . . In each case a well-known incumbent (Dukakis locally, Bush nationally) held on to a core of supporters ranging from 35 percent to 40 percent of the primary electorate. Iowa victories helped their challengers close this gap substantially, but not entirely." Lichter makes similar arguments for Jesse Jackson's momentum and the effects of Super Tuesday (an informal regional primary involving twenty-one jurisdictions).[11] The 1988 election did not disconfirm the conventional wisdom about the front-loaded character of the primary season. It only showed that momentum, while always a powerful factor, has limits.

Some might argue that my proposal is unnecessary: the entire spectacle of the present primary system on national television enables electorates in the later states to learn about the candidates in much the same way as a deliberative opinion poll would. Note, first, that if such a learning process were to occur, it would be filtered through the media rather than resulting from face-to-face interaction with the candidates. Second, it should be noted that candidate selection is generally decided before the later primaries, by which time many of the original candidates have been eliminated. Third, there is little indication that the rest of the nation learns much from the spectacle of the early primaries. Scott Keeter and Cliff Zukin point out that New Jersey voters, who stand late in the queue of primaries, show almost no learning about the candidates as the primary process unfolds. The curves for the percentages of voters who expressed no opinion about the various candidates in 1980 are almost flat from before the Iowa caucuses through June. Close to 60 percent had no opinion about candidate George Bush at the beginning and about the same had no opinion at the end. A similar pattern held true for Ronald Reagan, John Anderson, and others. Although some candidates had more opinions formed about them, this mostly reflected preexisting assets of name recognition rather than learning throughout the season.[12] The primary season is largely an unfolding process of non-opinion formation. It is not very deliberative at the beginning and not much more deliberative throughout. We see momentum without learning; choice without deliberation.

Given the continuing role of momentum during the primary season, a deliberative opinion poll would provide a better platform for launching candidacies than either the Iowa caucuses or the New Hampshire primary. Who can tell how a Bruce Babbitt or a Pete Du Pont might have done in a National Caucus? In any case, the states later in the queue, with different issues and populations, did not have a chance to give them serious consideration in 1988. And early winners will continue to calculate that they can benefit from the 1976 Carter strategy—a strategy focused on front-loading to attempt to break from the pack at the beginning.

Under the present system, who makes the initial choice for the rest of us? Two states that have almost no minority populations and that lack the urban concentrations of the nation's megastates. Of course, this problem could be remedied, in theory, by putting different states at the beginning of the primary process. But once we begin to think seriously about the issue, deeper problems emerge.

To indulge an analogy, let us distinguish among wholesale politics, mass-retail politics, and small-scale politics. When the candidates compete in a Super Tuesday, attempting to cover twenty-one jurisdictions with limited campaign resources in a short time, they can only engage in *wholesale* politics. They buy whatever television advertising they can afford and spread it thinly over a vast population. They flit from airport to airport just to make brief, smiling appearances on the evening news that have virtually no substantive content. And they hope that their opponents will make some mistake or that they can somehow get as much free media attention as possible.

Mass-retail politics is the special merit of Iowa and New Hampshire. The candidates make many visits, they shake many hands, they engage in many local debates. The advertising for the serious candidates achieves enough critical mass that the electorates in those states have a chance, if they are motivated, to associate names with faces and, perhaps, to develop comparatively informed opinions. Yet the claim that Iowa and New Hampshire offer "retail" politics rather than the new wholesale politics of the mass media is only a matter of degree. "Like other states," Gary Orren and Nelson Polsby note, "New Hampshire has become a 'media state.' New Hampshire voters learn about the campaign in their state by watching television, listening to the radio, and reading newspapers and magazines." Furthermore, the process in New Hampshire is more and more subject to media-generated momentum. "Increasingly, the candidates' standings in New Hampshire depend on how the media interpret the candidates' performance in Iowa," they conclude. "Momentum or bandwagon effects, where a candidate portrayed in the media as viable and improving begins to attract more support, are now crucial to the New Hampshire primary."[13] Retail politics in New Hampshire does not define an independent deliberative event but is, rather, largely determined by the media in New Hampshire and by media reactions to Iowa and to the earlier jockeying of the invisible primary. Clearly, if there were a different manner of launching the whole process, a deliberative prelude to the media-generated bandwagon, its momentum might have a major effect on Iowa, New Hampshire, and all that follows.

Events modeled on a deliberative opinion poll would provide a far more informed initial evaluation of candidates and issues. Such events would harness incentives for candidates—who, after all, are "issue entrepreneurs" with high visibility—to address and articulate the interests of every significant constituency in the country. Such events would constitute a kind of national laboratory for the growth of new issues as well as for the emergence of new candidates. Some of those issues can be expected to prove viable outside the laboratory—they will take on lives of their own in the succeeding months. Since the issues in presidential campaigns set the terms of debate for a large part of our political system, a more carefully designed collective experiment for launching issues in presidential campaigns makes sense. This proposal is intended to adapt the deliberative possibilities of *small-scale* politics to the problem of selecting candidates and launching issues in a large-scale nation-state.

Small-scale democracy permits a politics of face-to-face interaction, not mediated by newspapers or television. The delegates to a deliberative opinion poll would see what the candidates were like, shorn of their standard stump speeches (since, with repeated informal appearances to the same audience, they could not give the same speech over and over), shorn of media packaging for television, and shorn of "spin doctors" to implant favorable interpretations in news stories. It is as if the delegates were in *The Wizard of Oz*, and they all had the chance to go behind the screen and see what their aspiring national leaders were really like—without the hocus pocus and amplification they like to use to reach ordinary folk.

In a deliberative opinion poll, the first evaluation of candidates would have the thoughtfulness and depth of face-to-face politics, as well as the representative character of a national event that includes us all. It offers a way out of the false dilemma within which previous reforms have been trapped. It is not elitist; a deliberative opinion poll is representative of ordinary citizens. But it permits the reflectiveness of small-scale interactions to replace the comparative superficialities of mass-retail and wholesale politics.

Why would ordinary citizens take the time and trouble to participate in a deliberative opinion poll? First, the media could be expected to dramatize the process so much that most citizens would be glad of the opportunity to play a serious role in important historical events. Second, the delegates would be at least minimally compensated for their time. Events of this kind must be set up so that it is possible for any delegates selected to participate regardless of economic background. A third point is that the role of delegate should be considered analogous to that of juror. If this kind of event were eventually institutionalized, it should come to be considered an obligation of citizenship. The analogy between deliberative opinion polls and a jury is instructive in several respects. Both are meant, in some sense, to be representative of ordinary citizens. Both are premised on the notion that ordinary citizens, when immersed in the relevant materials, can deal with difficult intellectual questions. And it goes without saying in both cases that any attempts to fix the results or bribe the participants must be prevented by every possible means.

Rival proposals for reform are caught in the old dilemma: a forced choice between politically equal but relatively incompetent masses and politically unequal but relatively more competent elites. For example, if we were to cure the unrepresentative character of Iowa and New Hampshire by replacing the entire system with a "national primary," we would get only the thin reflectiveness of wholesale politics and large-scale mass democracy. It would be virtually impossible for new candidates to emerge. And the advantage of old ones would be based primarily on name recognition and on resources accumulated for television advertising. The real initial winnowing would probably be accomplished, to a considerable degree, by financial contributors before the official event. With little chance for questioning, interaction, or information, mass publics could not be expected to make a national primary a deliberative event.

A second prominent proposal, regional primaries, combines the defects of the present system with those of a national primary. The ordering of regional primaries would produce the same problem as Iowa and New Hampshire. A portion of the country, unrepresentative of the whole, would do the initial winnowing of candidates for the rest of us. Whichever region we selected, it would be inherently unrepresentative of the rest of the country. Primaries in the 1988 presidential season showed the power of regional identifications—for Albert Gore in the South, for Michael Dukakis in New England, and for George Bush in all the places he chooses to call home. Given the effects of earlier victories on later ones, the ordering of regional primaries would have a large and arbitrary influence on the outcome.

Former Vice President Walter Mondale has proposed that we deal with this issue by choosing the order of six regional primaries by lot.[14] However, some candidates would still have an enormous advantage simply because their region happened to go first. Instead of giving everyone the same starting point, this proposal would, in effect, give some runners in the race a big head start based on a lottery ticket. Rather than choosing a mass of delegates by lottery, a process with statistically predictable results for a group of decision-makers with specified characteristics, such a proposal for a lottery ordering of regional primaries would be more akin to our choosing a single chief executive by lottery—a prospect laden with risk. Given the crucial characteristics we need in one particular leader, such a proposal would have little to recommend it. Rather than using randomness to serve political equality, it would use randomness merely to serve arbitrariness in the selection process.

Most important, campaigns in regional primaries would have to be thinly spread in order to cover any large portion of the

country. The dialogue would be reduced to the smiles and simplifications of wholesale politics. Even sustained television advertising would be difficult over the whole region. And the
choices of campaign contributors *before* the first regional primary would, again, be decisive in determining the viability of
candidates.

Another prominent proposal, by the political scientists
Thomas Cronin and Robert Loevy, is that a national convention
be held first (with delegates chosen at state caucuses) to select
the candidates who would then be entitled to compete in a
"national primary."[15] But the effect of such a convention would
be to return power to the hands of party elites. They would do
the initial winnowing and the national primary (to choose
among the elite-sanctioned candidates) would have all the familiar thinness of wholesale politics. It is arguable that this
inventive proposal, rather than solving our dilemma, is vulnerable to both horns of the dilemma simultaneously. On the one
hand, it seems antidemocratic because of the dominant role it
gives to party elites. On the other hand, it offers the thin mass
democracy of a national primary.

A similar point can be made about the political scientist
Everett Carl Ladd's proposal that a national primary be combined with a requirement that the party conventions set aside
one-third of their delegate seats for party officials and elected
officeholders. Although Ladd argues for "peer review" and more
effective deliberation at the convention,[16] it is hard to imagine
that the winners of such a system would not effectively be determined by the national primary. As we will see, direct-
majoritarian institutions such as primaries have great legitimacy in the current state of American political culture. The
winner of a national primary would have the blessings of the
people as presented and interpreted by national television. Party
officials would find it difficult to resist the bandwagon produced
by such a mandate. Yet a national primary, as we have already
seen, has all the disadvantages of a giant Super Tuesday. Preexisting name recognition, credibility with fund-raisers, manipulation of television advertising, momentum in the invisible

primary, and all the other familiar features of the present system would apply. Clearly, some quite different approach is needed if a way is to be found out of our basic dilemma. The only innovation in the two hybrid proposals just considered (from Cronin/Loevey and Ladd) is that they might well offer us *both* horns of our dilemma, both political inequality and impaired deliberation, simultaneously.

A deliberative opinion poll is not an organ of the party professionals. It would use the sampling techniques of public opinion research to represent, to make present, a version of all of us. It is ironic that the banes of wholesale mass democracy—continuous opinion polling and market research—led to the perfection of sampling techniques that can now be harnessed for a more meaningful form of democracy.

The deliberative opinion poll is only one of several possible innovations that can help us achieve both political equality and deliberation. By itself, it is only one step. It is certainly far from being a panacea for the problems of the American political system. We need a new research agenda for the general class of innovations that might bring "power to the people" under conditions where the people could exercise their power more thoughtfully. In a time of experimentation with democracy around the world, we need to connect anew with both the spirit of innovation and the fuller vision of democracy that animated the Founders. Although we have experimented a great deal with our democratic institutions, that experimentation has largely been driven by an overly constrained vision of democratic possibilities. I will attempt to sketch here a more complete map of democratic alternatives—one that will help us chart directions toward more adequate democratic reforms.

I will argue that a fully defensible version of democracy must simultaneously fulfill three conditions: it must achieve political equality, its decisions must embody deliberation, and it must avoid tyranny of the majority. As we will see, each of these conditions raises difficult issues. Yet neglect of any one of them produces decisive objections. The problem with recent reforms is that they aspire to political equality at the cost of deliberation. Yet this pattern, while crucially important in recent times, particularly in the United States, is only one of the possible pathologies that can emerge in democratic reforms. This book is offered as a first step toward a more adequate theory of democracy that might provide the basis for more inspiring strategies of democratic reform.

Size and Democracy

2 Democracy is spreading throughout the world. In the latter part of the twentieth century, we tend to take its appropriateness for granted. Yet until the late eighteenth century, democracy was thought to be inapplicable to the large-scale nation-state. It was a form of government appropriate for city-states or small republics. Rousseau thought the conditions for democracy were most favorable in his native Geneva, which in his time had a population of about twenty-two thousand. Aristotle, no friend of democracy, had previously noted that it was limited to states where all citizens could gather and still hear a speaker—a highly restrictive definition in an age that lacked modern technology.[1]

In discussing limits of size, Aristotle prescribed that "both in order to give decisions in matters of disputed rights and to distribute the offices of government according to the merit of the candidates, the citizens of a state must know one anothers' characters." If a state is too large, "who can give it orders, unless he has Stentor's voice?" In discussing the limits of size imposed even by the rule of law, Aristotle makes clear that too large a society throws the issue outside his ken. "The creation of order for an infinite number is a task for the divine power."[2]

The American Founders launched a brave and, many thought, foolhardy experiment in attempting to establish popular government in such a large state. They even struggled for terminology to express the sense in which they aspired to some form of popular government, a "democratic republic" or perhaps a "representative democracy."[3] Even more important, they were well aware that the lessons of history did not seem to be on their side. In *Federalist* no. 14, James Madison is almost plaintive in his appeal to his readers: "Harken not

to the voice which petulantly tells you that the form of government recommended for your adoption is a novelty in the political world; that it has never yet had a place in the theories of the
wildest projectors; that it rashly attempts what it is impossible
to accomplish."[4]

Concerned to resist those who would argue that a democratic
republic is possible only on a small scale, Madison challenges
them to think what it would mean to break up the American
states in order to reduce them to a manageable size: "And if
novelties are to be shunned, believe me, the most alarming of all
novelties, the most wild of all projects, the most rash of all
attempts, is that of rending us in pieces in order to preserve our
liberties and promote our happiness." He is willing to embrace
the newness of the effort to bring popular government to a large-
scale republic, even though the proposed system has few historical parallels. Madison tells us not to reject "the experiment of
an extended republic . . . merely because it may comprise what
is new." It is "the glory of the people of America" that "they
have not suffered a blind veneration for antiquity, for custom, or
for names, to overrule the suggestions of their own good sense."[5]

In the eighteenth century it was generally believed that representative institutions could not function in a large, extended
state. Patrick Henry, for example, predicted "that one government cannot reign over so extensive a territory as this is without
absolute despotism."[6] Similar views about the inevitability of
monarchy in some form, if not dictatorship, had been previously
expressed by both John Adams and Alexander Hamilton.[7]

Montesquieu was the canonical source for this view about
size limits, and he was invoked by both sides in the debate. He
held that "it is natural for a republic to have only a small territory; otherwise it cannot long subsist." Only in a small republic
would it be possible for the public interest to be understood. "In
an extensive republic the public good is sacrificed to a thousand
private views," Montesquieu argued. "It is subordinate to exceptions and depends on accidents. In a small one, the interest of
the public is more obvious, better understood, and more within

the reach of every citizen; abuses have less extent, and, of course, are less protected."[8]

Montesquieu also argued that Sparta succeeded partly because the number of its citizens had been limited to ten thousand, while Rome fell partly because it let the number of its citizens expand: "Rome, I say, never fixed the number; and this was one of the principal causes of its ruin."[9]

In this context, Madison's argument in *Federalist* no. 10 that an "extended republic" might offer a more promising prospect for popular government than a small republic, was a remarkable departure. We now know that Madison was inspired by Hume to turn Montesquieu on his head. In the "Idea of a Perfect Commonwealth," Hume had argued that "in a large government . . . there is compass and room enough to refine the democracy."[10] Hume proposed a complex system of indirect elections where local elections would determine countywide electors who would, in turn, elect senators. In such an indirect federal system, "the parts are so distant and remote that it is very difficult, either by intrigue, prejudice, or passion, to hurry them into any measures against the public interest." Here was a perception that tyranny might better be avoided in a large, complex, and indirect system than in a small, direct one.

Madison developed this insight in *Federalist* no. 10, where he argued that there are two chief differences between a "pure democracy," by which he meant a direct democracy, and the other possible form of popular government, a "republic." The first crucial difference is that a republic employs representatives. This makes it possible to "refine and enlarge the public views by passing them through a chosen body of citizens." Hence, representation may make possible greater deliberation. Second, there is "the greater number of citizens and extent of territory which may be brought within the compass of republican than of democratic government." Madison then develops his famous argument that in an extended republic "you take in a greater variety of parties and interests; you make it less probable that a majority of the whole will have a common motive to invade the rights of other citizens." He offers a number of probabilistic arguments as to why this proposition might be true.[11] The burden of the second argument is that in an extended republic, tyranny of the majority will be less likely than in a small, direct democracy where the passions of the people can be immediately aroused. Madison is arguing that an extended republic can serve the ultimate aim of achieving a nontyrannous and deliberative form of popular government.

Hence, two of Madison's central values were deliberation and nontyranny. Elsewhere he argued for a third, which I will call political equality. He attacked the rotten boroughs of the British parliamentary system and the corruption fostered by grossly unequal election districts.[12] My exploration here will focus on these same three values—political equality, deliberation, and nontyranny. As did the Federalists, I will take the main problem of constitutional theory to be the adaptation of democracy to the large-scale nation-state in such a form that it achieves all three of these values.

Hamilton pointed out that even the current American states were too large to satisfy Montesquieu. "When Montesquieu recommends a small extent for republics," Hamilton argues in *Federalist* no. 9, "the standards he had in view were of dimensions far short of the limits of almost every one of these States. Neither Virginia, Massachusetts, Pennsylvania, New York, North Carolina, nor Georgia can by any means be compared with the models from which he reasoned."[13] If the scale argument were to be taken seriously, the American states would "be driven to the alternative either of taking refuge at once in the arms of monarchy, or of splitting ourselves into an infinity of little, jealous, clashing commonwealths." Hamilton then turned Montesquieu against his opponents by pointing out that the Frenchman also advocated a "confederate republic" that would combine a number of small republics. Ignoring the fact that the examples cited by Montesquieu involved a far looser confederation than the one envisioned in the proposed American constitution,[14] and that he had just argued that the American states were already too large by Montesquieu's standards, Hamilton offered the notion of a confederate republic as proof

that even the champions of small-scale democracy could subscribe to the plan proposed.

However, the champions of small-scale democracy had a different agenda, which found expression in the diverse group of
writers who have come to be known as the Anti-Federalists. As
with Montesquieu, their central tenet was that a small society
was the only appropriate site for a republic. "At the center" of
their view was "the belief that republican government was possible only for a relatively small territory and a relatively small
and homogeneous population."[15] They were animated by a vision of direct democracy or, as second best, a small democracy
kept as close to the people as possible. Hence, for those who
admitted the need for representatives "as a substitute for the
meeting together of all the citizens," the point was "to keep the
representatives directly answerable to and dependent on their
constituents. This is the reason for the concern with short
terms of office, frequent rotation, and a numerous representation."[16]

The direct-majoritarian vision that animated the Anti-
Federalists, while it lost the initial battle over the Constitution,
has largely won the war in the long march of history—the war to
determine the vision of legitimate politics directing change in
American democracy. As we will see, many changes, both formal and informal, have taken us closer and closer to a direct-
majoritarian version of democracy. The modern presumption
has become that anything more direct and majoritarian must be
more democratic than institutional patterns that allow leaders
to retain discretion or to be elected less directly. Hence, referendums and primaries are thought to express a superior form of
democracy to that expressed by legislative decisions and selection of candidates by party leaders or state conventions. When
leaders go against popular preferences reported in opinion polls,
this is thought to be antidemocratic as well. A plebiscitary
model of leadership is coming to displace the more complex
vision of democracy that animated the Founders. Shorn of its
connection to small-scale democracy, a connection born of the
Athenian Assembly and asserted by the Anti-Federalists, this

vision of direct-majoritarianism has been transformed into a popular ideology for the large-scale nation-state. In this transformation, the face-to-face character of deliberation possible in the small-scale version has dropped out;[17] it has been replaced by millions of atomistic citizens who bounce back unreflective preferences from the mass media. A distorted version of the Anti-Federalist vision has worked its way into most of our institutions. As Giovanni Sartori has argued, our democratic institutions have become something of an echo chamber. "The daily bombardment with and by polls has brought about a 'poll-direction' . . . which is nothing other than a reflection-effect, or an echo-effect, of what the media themselves have been suggesting."[18] Instead of public opinions worthy of the name controlling leaders, preferences shaped by leaders and by the mass media too often are bounced back, reflected in polls, without sufficient critical scrutiny and without sufficient information and examination to represent any meaningful popular control.[19]

Perhaps Michael Oreskes put it best in a remarkable series in the *New York Times* describing widespread disaffection from our system of campaigns and elections. "An unhappy consensus has emerged," he argues, "that domestic politics has become so shallow, mean and even meaningless that it is failing to produce the ideas and the leadership needed to guide the United States in a rapidly changing world. . . . Trivialization. Atomization. Paralysis. These words have become the descriptive vocabulary on which members of both parties draw to describe the state of politics and government in America."[20]

To the extent that this charge is true, I would argue that much of the blame rests on the power of an idea—a too limited vision of democracy. Since the founding of the republic, it has guided numerous transformations of both formal institutions and informal practices in American politics. These changes have, of course, not been motivated merely by a normative vision. All such changes depend on changes in society, in technology, and on the operation of many incentives, both institutional and personal. Nevertheless, we need to connect the research agenda of institutional changes with a fuller consideration of the values at stake in a truly adequate version of democracy. The three values already noted in Madison's writing—deliberation, non-tyranny, and political equality—will guide our inquiry. Pursuit of a direct-majoritarian vision reminiscent of the Anti-Federalists has led us to empty the system of effective deliberation by bringing power to the masses under conditions where the masses have little chance to deliberate about the power they exercise. In envisioning reformulations of democracy for the large-scale nation-state, reformulations that might better achieve all three of the values just identified, I am only proposing that we continue the spirit of innovation launched by the Founders. We must put true democratization in the place of what Robert Dahl has recently called "pseudodemocratization," a notion he applied to the presidency to mean "a change taken with the ostensible, and perhaps even actual, purpose of enhancing the democratic process that in practice retains the aura of its democratic justification and yet has the effect, intended or unintended, of weakening the democratic process."[21] Of course, to apply such a term we need to specify carefully what might be meant by an enhancement or a weakening of the democratic process. The agenda of this book is, first, to supply a theoretical framework, a map of possibilities intended to do just that, and, second, to apply that map to actual changes which have taken place, and which might be prescribed, for the American political system and other experiments in democracy throughout the world.

The Lure of Direct Democracy

3 Suppose we hooked up the entire American electorate to a two-way cable system such as the Warner-Amex Qube (a television system that enables people to vote in their homes). If we were inspired by the image of direct-majoritarian control of public policy, we could use such a system to institute a "teledemocracy."[1] To fulfill this vision, we need not replace all our representative institutions. Perhaps we could keep the Congress as an agenda setter. Congressional committees might be employed to refine proposals that would be put, in a constant stream, in competition before the electorate after the evening news. Perhaps other proposals would be put to a vote if they were supported by a certain number of petition signatures. The Executive Branch and the Judiciary could operate much as before, but the legislative function would be in the ultimate hands of the public speaking through the Qube.

The "Simple Qube" system represents the final aspiration of a certain limited vision of democracy. If we were to take it seriously, it would arouse two decisive objections. First, the deliberative competence of mass publics is suspect. It is a dubious accomplishment to give power to the people under conditions where they are not really in a position to think about how they are to exercise that power. Second, aroused publics might, on occasion, be vulnerable to demagoguery. They might be stirred up to invade the rights or trample on the essential interests of minorities. If a simple vote of mass publics after the nightly news were the only prerequisite for new legislation, there would be few impediments to tyranny of the majority once the public was aroused.

The Simple Qube model realizes too thin a notion of democracy. Suppose, however, that we were to modify the Qube so that it was hooked up, not to the entire electorate, but only to *representative samples* of the electorate. We might suppose that each such sample was transitory, so that there was no question that members of the sample group would differ in their deliberations from the electorate at large. Suppose, furthermore, that our customary representative institutions appeared to function in the familiar way, except that each legislator received instructions from representative samples of the relevant electorate (drawn from the appropriate congressional district for a congressman, from the appropriate state for a senator, or from the entire nation for the president). Perhaps we would allow the political actor, in each case, to formulate the poll questions put to the relevant Qube sample in asking for instructions. Hence, the poll results would be open to a certain degree of manipulation and interpretation. If we call the earlier model the Simple Qube system, we might call this variation the "Representative Qube" system.

The Representative Qube system is not fundamentally different from the Simple Qube system. Representatives would take their instructions from the relevant polls. Although they would have some opportunities for manipulating the results by formulating the poll questions, and although they would be bound by public opinion in constituencies smaller than the national electorate, there would be no pretension that these political actors were deliberative agents.

With the appropriate statistical techniques, it should not matter that only a small sample of the electorate would be hooked up in the Representative Qube, rather than the entire electorate, as in the Simple Qube. If the sampling were done properly, it would have little statistical likelihood of making a difference. The same basic objections that apply to the Simple Qube system apply to the Representative Qube system. Lack of deliberation and vulnerability to tyranny of the majority would make either a questionable realization of the democratic idea.

Now let us imagine a third model, which I will call the "Plebiscitary Model." In this system, there is no actual Qube hook-up. Instead, there is only a stream of actual opinion polls taken by many different agents. Political actors do not, however, view themselves as bound by any particular opinion poll. Instead, they act with reference to the *shared public estimate of an imaginary opinion poll*, an imaginary plebiscite. That opinion poll is the one that would be taken on the issues *framed in the way the political actor would like to persuade the public that it ought to be framed*. In the Plebiscitary Model, actions by the politician can be explained largely in two ways: as efforts to get the public to frame the issues in the shared imaginary opinion poll in the way the politician finds favorable to his or her cause; or as efforts by the politician to do as well as possible in the shared imaginary opinion poll by persuading the public and other actors that his or her position is to be preferred.

The imaginary opinion poll is the shared perception of how well the political actor is doing in an imaginary plebiscite, a plebiscite that is normally not precisely the same as any actual poll. But all of the actual polls can be used as rough indicators, as snapshots from distorted angles, of how the plebiscite would probably come out if it were held at any one time.

When a politician acts in the way just described, I will say that he or she is conforming to the Plebiscitary Model. If the Representative Qube system is not too different in its basic results from the Simple Qube system, it also seems to be the case that the Plebiscitary Model is not too different in its ultimate effects from the Representative Qube.

Actors in our political system do not now fully conform to the Plebiscitary Model. But they have been moving closer to it. Many changes in behavior by our most important political actors should be seen as ever closer approximations. These informal changes, when combined with many explicit legal and constitutional changes, have moved us closer to mimicking the effects of a democracy which is far more direct than we usually acknowledge.

The Plebiscitary Model is being spread worldwide by public opinion polling. It should not be assumed that informal movement toward the Plebiscitary Model is limited to systems that have consolidated a democratic transition. It is possible for elements of it to be important even in authoritarian regimes—provided that political leaders have some reason (perhaps fear of mass disaffection or mass disruption) to be solicitous of public opinion. Eduard Shevardnadze, for example, pioneered the use of public opinion polls among the Communist party bosses when he was First Party Secretary of the Communist party of Soviet Georgia from 1972 to 1985.[2] Mikhail Gorbachev, himself, is known to make considerable use of opinion polls. Another important element of the Plebiscitary Model was introduced when Gorbachev's standing in the polls began to be regularly published.[3]

The basic difficulty is that the vision of democracy needed to support the Plebiscitary Model is incomplete. In this time of international ferment in the realization of democracy, it is imperative to begin operating with more than half a vision of democratic possibilities.

The half-vision that has dominated recent discussion can be characterized as direct-majoritarianism. Anything that causes the system to conform better to our shared perception of majority opinion, and anything that supplants effective decisionmaking at the representative level with effective decision making by the people themselves, comes to be perceived as more democratic. Hence, primaries are thought to be more democratic than party caucuses or state conventions, referendums are thought to be more democratic than legislative decisions, deference to opinion polls is thought to be more democratic than a representative's considered judgment that he or she should depart from the poll. Many of our constitutional amendments and formal political changes have also brought clear movement in this direction. But many of the most important movements in the direct-majoritarian direction have been informal. Hence my emphasis on the partial adoption of something approximating the Plebiscitary Model as a strategy of political leadership. Such informal changes can be found in the presidency, the Congress, and many other political roles, such as governorships and state legislatures.

There is widely perceived legitimacy in the notion of democracy that would justify the Plebiscitary Model and its variations—direct primaries and referendums. But this notion of democracy neglects the deliberation needed to make democratic choices meaningful. We have moved to achieve political equality, but at the cost of sacrificing deliberation.[4] This essay is intended to outline the conditions for a fuller vision of democracy that would achieve both political equality and deliberation. This quest will lead us to investigate, first, how we have found ourselves choosing between political equality and deliberation, and, second, how new forms of representation might be designed to attain both objectives.

Through informal approximations to the Plebiscitary Model, through formal legal changes, through changes in party rules and practices, we have been moving to realize a more direct, more majoritarian democracy so as to empty the process of deliberation. Until now, it has seemed as if we must choose between the political equality aspired to by direct-majoritarian democracy and the deliberation fostered by representative institutions. However, this dilemma is false. We have only a brief history of experimenting with the adaptations of democracy to the large-scale nation-state. There is plenty of room for innovations that could overcome our present dilemmas of democratic reform.

Part Two
Democracy in Three Dimensions

Three Democratic Conditions
Political Equality, Nontyranny, and Deliberation

4 Our ideal image of democracy requires that three separate conditions be satisfied. Institutional arrangements that satisfy one or, at most, two of these conditions have tended to undermine the rest. By concentrating on *partial* pictures of what democracy ought to be, we have brought about changes that often do at least as much harm as good. Yet, I will argue, it would not be impossible to bring about reforms that further all three conditions at once.

The three essential conditions for a fully realized democratic system are political equality, nontyranny, and deliberation. Without political equality, votes are not counted equally or the voices of some do not get an effective hearing. Without nontyranny, the essential interests of some groups are destroyed when such outcomes could be entirely avoided for everyone. In other words, when tyranny of the majority is the result, the moral claims of democracy are undermined. Without deliberation, democratic choices are not exercised in a meaningful way. If the preferences that determine the results of democratic procedures are unreflective or ignorant, then they lose their claim to political authority over us. Deliberation is necessary if the claims of democracy are not to be de-legitimated.

Political Equality
Efforts to realize political equality have to be evaluated both in terms of the formal decision-rules employed and in terms of the background conditions that set the stage for participation in those formal decision-rules. If the votes of people in one region or from one racial or ethnic group do not count in the same way as those from another region or racial or ethnic group, then there is a clear violation of formal political equal-

29

ity. If one representative has a hundred thousand constituents and another has, say, five million, then we know that the voters in the larger district are not getting their fair share of representation in the legislature. But votes could count equally in a formal sense and the results might still violate political equality. Suppose that supporters of a single dominant party control the media and access to them, and criticisms from the organized opposition never get a hearing. Suppose further that the mass media are the predominant means of access to influence over public opinion. If the dominant party wins election after election with all votes counting equally, we might, nevertheless, question the extent to which the system realized political equality. This example illustrates one way in which background fairness might be violated.

Consider another. Suppose there is a long-standing practice of political clientalism whereby certain rich and influential notables customarily tell the voters in a district how to vote. The deliberative process of mass individualized voting decisions is, in other words, completely short-circuited. To please the local notable the voters, by and large, simply do as they are told. We might imagine that their jobs depend on it. Or we might imagine that it is a religious notable and they believe their chances for salvation hinge on whether they obey the dictates of their leader. Or we might imagine that they are simply bribed. In these latter cases, extreme economic and social inequalities spill over onto the political process, destroying any opportunity for individual deliberation. Even if the procedural fairness required by formal political equality or equal voting power were fully implemented, it would hardly seem plausible to say that such cases satisfied a fully adequate account of political equality. The election would be unfair in just the same way as if some people had grossly unequal voting power in the formal decision-rule.

These different cases suggest several related factors that must be satisfied. By political equality I mean *the institutionalization of a system which grants equal consideration to everyone's preferences and which grants everyone appropriately equal op-*

portunities to formulate preferences on the issues under consideration. Because granting equal consideration has two components, the full notion of political equality yields three separate requirements. First, there must be formal equality granting equal weight to peoples' preferences on, for example, candidates or parties to be selected in an election, or the issues in a referendum. Second, there must be guarantees that the political process has not been interfered with by irrelevant factors. If, for example, the election has been bought, then there has been a failure in terms of the second requirement, which I will call the insulation condition. The political sphere must be protected from being determined by spillover effects from social or economic inequalities in the society. Third, there must be adequate opportunities for voters to form preferences. If, for example, everyone were brainwashed to defer to the established political leadership, then the existence of formal political equality and of insulation conditions would not be enough to guarantee political equality. Given appropriate background conditions of education preparing everyone for some minimal degree of autonomous citizenship,[1] the important point here is what I will call an effective hearing. The major rival viewpoints must get enough of a hearing that people have the opportunity to decide among them. On this analysis, then, political equality requires implementation of three components: (a) formal political equality, (b) insulation conditions, and (c) an effective hearing. It is worth discussing each of these conditions in turn.

By formal political equality, I mean a procedure which gives equal consideration to the preferences of each citizen. A rigorous definition can be taken from indexes for equal voting power such as the Shapely-Shubik or Banzhaf indexes.[2] The basic idea is that formal political equality is achieved when every voter has an equal probability of being the decisive voter, assuming that we know nothing about the actual distribution of preferences of the other voters (and so that every alternative is equally likely). This definition captures the root notion of various formal indexes for equal voting power. It applies to proportional representation, majority rule in equal population districts, random samples, lottery systems, and many other devices that have been employed or debated.[3]

Madison, in *Federalist* no. 56, illustrates the dangers of violating formal political equality. The number of inhabitants of England and Scotland, Madison calculates, "cannot be stated at less than eight millions. The representatives of these eight millions in the House of Commons amount to five hundred and fifty eight. Of this number, one ninth are elected by three hundred and sixty-four persons and one half, by five thousand seven hundred and twenty-three persons."[4]

This situation leads to inattention, lack of responsiveness, and often corruption on the part of the half of the legislators who are chosen by such a small number of persons. "It cannot be supposed," Madison continues, "that the half thus elected . . . can add anything to the security of the people against the government, or to the knowledge of their circumstances and interests in the legislative councils." Quite the contrary, "it is notorious that they are more frequently the representatives and instruments of the executive magistrate than the guardians and advocates of the popular rights."[5]

However, Madison was aware of the need to avoid not only numerical inequality but also political corruption. "English experience with parliamentary corruption had been decisive for Madison," Robert J. Morgan argues. "If patronage and other 'vicious arts' were used in elections, one group might be served at the expense of others."[6]

While gross formal political inequality may, as Madison contended, facilitate corruption and other spillover effects from economic and social inequalities onto the political sphere, the spillover effects may occur without the formal inequality.

Hence, we are led to our second requirement—insulation conditions. By this I mean that threats or bargains outside the political sphere should not decisively determine results within the political sphere. For example, people's votes should not be determined by expectations of employment or by fear that they will be fired if they vote the wrong way. Similarly, their votes should not be determined by threats of coercion or by promised rewards in an afterlife. If political results are determined by offers of reward or threats of negative consequences offered by those who occupy favored positions in the socioeconomic structure, then the power of those favored positions is spilling over onto the political sphere in such a way that we can say that there has been a failure of the insulation condition.

The third requirement for political equality is an effective hearing for the full range of interests that have significant followings—in a deliberative setting where the decision making, constrained by formal equality, may in principle be influenced by the effective hearing.[7] In the United States, our representative institutions embody, at best, a kind of distorted political equality. It is distorted, first, because, despite the one-person–one-vote reforms launched by the courts since *Baker v. Carr*, we do not have equal voting power (notably in the U.S. Senate); and, second, it is distorted because many interests do not get an effective hearing. Our system of campaign financing requires that huge sums of money be raised to pay for television time. Political action committees and corporate contributions serve to distort access to the media in a perpetual campaign environment.[8]

More needs to be said about the notion of an effective hearing. Clearly, if some groups are silenced or forcibly prevented from speaking, then they have been denied an effective hearing. However, the system of free expression cannot be evaluated merely in terms of whether some positions are forcibly suppressed. Crucial voices may fail to achieve an effective hearing without the need to silence any of them. In a modern, technologically complex society, access to the mass media is a necessary condition for a voice to contribute to the national political debate. Unless the media permit the full range of views that have a significant following in the society to get access to the media on issues of intense interest to proponents of those views, then the full realization of political equality has fallen short.

There is considerable room for debate about what might count as a view with a "significant following" and what might count as an issue of "intense interest" to those who hold such a view. For our purposes here, we do not need to set any particular threshold or any particular standard for measurement. The few empirical references we will make to the notion are clear enough cases that they would be counted as problems for an effective hearing on any reasonable construction. At this stage, I only need to establish the principle that if groups are frozen out of the debate on issues about which they feel intensely, there comes a point when political equality has been undermined— no matter how perfectly the mathematical properties of the voting system achieve equality in a formal index of voting power.

Nontyranny

By tyranny I mean the choice of a policy that imposes severe deprivations when an alternative policy could have been chosen that would have imposed no severe deprivations on anyone. By severe deprivation, I mean the destruction of essential human interests. In *Tyranny and Legitimacy,* I adopted one particular definition of severe deprivations.[9] But we do not need to settle the issue here of what we might mean by the destruction of essential human interests. Any of the consequences that might qualify as denials of basic human rights will do. When the survival or the bases of fundamental human dignities are denied, then severe deprivations have been imposed. A policy choice may be considered tyrannous if it imposes such deprivations when an alternative policy could have been chosen that would have imposed them on no one. The avoidance of tyranny can be considered a necessary condition for an acceptable form of democracy.

When the Nazis perpetrated the Holocaust or when Idi Amin expelled the Asians from Uganda, these were tyrannous policy choices visited upon a portion of the population, since severe deprivations that destroyed essential human interests could have been avoided for everyone. No matter how popular some version of these terrible events may have been with some portions of the population, no defensible theory of democracy can legitimate such outcomes. These obvious cases will serve to illustrate the point that an acceptable theory of democracy must have a nontyranny constraint. For purposes of our argument here, you should feel free to fill in the account of essential human interests or of severe deprivations as you wish. What you regard as the most important human interests will determine your specific notion of a tyrannous policy choice. Because the dilemmas explored in the rest of my argument will focus on the conflict between deliberation and political equality, I will not discuss the notion of a tyrannous policy choice further here.

For the sake of completeness, however, the coequal status of the nontyranny condition, along with deliberation and political equality, must be mentioned. Without a nontyranny constraint, the normative theory of democracy is vulnerable to decisive counterexample. In some cases it might appear to legitimate what we would regard as tyranny of the majority. A systematic description of what should count as tyrannous policy choice arouses innumerable controversies. We need not, however, detain ourselves with them here. As long as the point is granted, in principle, that an adequate theory of democracy would include a nontyranny condition, we can move on to the issues of real concern for us. In any case, I have produced a full-scale attempt to spell out the nontyranny condition elsewhere.[10]

Deliberation

A significant strand of democratic theory would make distinctions among forms of public opinion. In one of the most famous examples, Madison argues in *Federalist* no. 10 that an extended republic should not take public opinion in its raw form. Rather, it was "to refine and enlarge the public views by passing them through the medium of a chosen body of citizens." The "public voice" arrived at by such representatives "will be more consonant to the public good than if pronounced by the people themselves, convened for the purpose."[11] Similarly, Hamilton, in *Federalist* no. 71, clearly distinguished the "temporary delusion" of "inclination" or "transient impulse" from the public's consideration of its interests when there was "opportunity for more cool and sedate reflection." According to Hamilton, "the

deliberate sense of the community should govern." His republican principle "does not require an unqualified complaisance to
every sudden breeze of passion or to every transient impulse
which the public may receive from the arts of men who flatter
their prejudices to betray their interests."[12]

This distinction between the inclinations of the moment and
public opinions that are refined by "sedate reflection" is an
essential part of any adequate theory of democracy. Political
equality without deliberation is not of much use, for it amounts
to nothing more than power without the opportunity to think
about how that power ought to be exercised. Something like the
criterion that Dahl labels "enlightened understanding" is required: "In order to express his or her preferences accurately,
each citizen ought to have adequate and equal opportunities for
discovering and validating, in the time permitted by the need for
a decision, what his or her preferences are on the matter to be
decided."[13]

Setting aside the practical constraint of the "time permitted
by the need for a decision," there is clearly an ideal of deliberation here which could be pushed further and which would take
us ultimately to something like the "ideal speech situation" of
Jurgen Habermas—a situation of free and equal discussion, unlimited in its duration, constrained only by the consensus
which would be arrived at by the "force of the better argument."[14] In the ideal speech situation, every argument thought
to be relevant by anyone would be given as extensive a hearing as
anyone wanted. If a conclusion could be reached without any
limit to decision-costs by free and equal persons, then that conclusion can be considered the ideally rational one.

The requirements of the ideal speech situation are, of course,
purely hypothetical and, in that sense, utterly utopian. A more
concrete but still utopian specification of a deliberative ideal for
collective decision making is offered by David Braybrooke in his
work on issue processing:

> In what we might define as logically complete debate, the
> participants, turn by turn, raise proposals and invoke argu-

ments for them; and the other participants deal with all the proposals and answer all the arguments not their own; thus as the issue moves toward resolution, every participant is aware at every stage of every ingredient still current in the debate—every proposal outstanding; the arguments still pressed on its behalf; the distribution among the participants of favor for the various proposals and of opposition to them, and as well the distribution of conviction respecting the various arguments and of doubt. Thus when the issue is resolved, say by a majority voting to adopt a certain set of proposals, every participant, whether in the majority or in the minority, will have the same complete information about the track that the debate has taken.[15]

It is worth adding that the participants must be willing to consider the arguments offered on their merits. They listen and participate with an openness to the reasons given on one side or another. Whether they will finally decide in terms of their personal interests or values or the interests or values of some group or region is left open by the notion of deliberation developed here.

With these caveats, we can think of Braybrooke's "logically complete debate" as the endpoint of a continuum that would be far out of reach for any actual deliberative body limited by what Dahl calls the "time permitted by the need for a decision." Yet as the ideal endpoint, it serves as an aspiration defining the outer limits of the deliberative dimension of the political process. Institutions and situations are closer to the nondeliberative end when they exhibit various forms of incompleteness— incompleteness in the arguments (thought to be relevant by one participant or another) that have not been expressed so that others are aware of them; incompleteness in the opportunities for the proponents of a position to answer the arguments expressed on behalf of rival positions; incompleteness in the knowledge or capacities of participants that would permit them to understand the arguments expressed on behalf of one position or another. We can consider situations that are more and more extreme in their incompleteness in one or another of these ways so that, at some point, we arrive at an endpoint of nondeliberation, an endpoint where an alternative is not contrasted effectively with its rivals, where arguments are not answered, and where the decision makers have little competence or factual background to evaluate the proposals offered to them. Given these two endpoints, my discussion of the deliberative dimension will, obviously, always be a matter of degree. I will sometimes speak of an institutional innovation serving deliberation when it falls far short of the ideal but nevertheless represents a significant improvement over the lack of deliberation that we routinely encounter at present.

From this perspective, John Stuart Mill can be treated as a theorist who was very concerned to achieve deliberation and nontyranny, and was willing to sacrifice political equality—at least at the level of the large-scale nation-state—in order to do so. Mill was concerned to protect the independence of legislators and to give extra influence to those with more mental competence.

The superior competence of legislators led him to a decided preference for representative over direct democracy. "When the value of knowledge is adequately felt, a man will choose his legislator as he chooses his physician," Mill speculates. "No man pretends to instruct his physician. No man exacts a pledge from his physician that he shall prescribe for him a particular treatment."[16] Similarly, Mill believes that legislators ought to have the discretion to make the best decision and the deference from ordinary citizens that we commonly grant to our physicians.

The effort to promote deliberation and mental competence in politics led Mill not only to advocate greater autonomy for legislators but also to grant extra influence, at the mass level, to those with greater competence. In this way, Mill was led to his notorious proposal for "plural voting." In this proposal, which would have granted extra weight to those with greater competence, "no one needs ever be called upon for a complete sacrifice of his own opinion," Mill assures us. "It can always be taken into the calculation, and counted at a certain figure, a higher figure being assigned to the suffrages of those whose opinion is entitled to greater weight."[17]

Mill considers granting extra votes to graduates of universities, to members of certain professions, or to those who can pass a certain kind of test. Whatever the precise institutional arrangement, "the only thing which can justify reckoning one person's opinion as equivalent to more than one is individual mental superiority and what is wanted is some approximate means for ascertaining that."[18] In the interest of achieving greater deliberation (and, he believed, of protecting against tyranny of the majority as well), Mill was quite willing to sacrifice political equality.

John C. Calhoun was another theorist who was willing to sacrifice political equality in order to facilitate both nontyranny and deliberation. Instead of relying on the "numerical majority" that would be the result of giving legislators equal voting power, he proposed a system of "concurrent majorities," in which majorities among each of the significant groups in the society would be necessary and where each such group would have a veto that could bring government to a halt. The veto was both a protection against tyranny and oppression and a spur to deliberation:

> The government of the concurrent majority, where the organism is perfect, excludes the possibility of oppression by giving to each interest, or portion, or order—where there are established classes—measures of protecting itself by its negative against all measures calculated to advance the peculiar interests of others at its expense. Its effect, then, is to cause the different interests, portions, or orders as the case may be . . . to unite in such measures only as would promote the prosperity of all, as the only means to prevent the suspension of the action of the government, and thereby to avoid anarchy—the greatest of all evils.[19]

Calhoun believed that the threat of anarchy—from the suspension of government action by the veto of one group or another—would produce deliberation.[20] The effort to avoid anarchy would focus everyone's attention on those measures which could serve the good of all: "No necessity can be more urgent and imperious than that of avoiding anarchy. . . . Traced to this source, the voice of a people—uttered under the necessity of avoiding the greatest of calamities through the organs of a government so constructed as to suppress the expression of all partial and selfish interests, and to give a full and faithful utterance to the sense of the whole community, in reference to the sense of the whole community, in reference to its common welfare—may without impiety, be called *the voice of God*."[21]

Calhoun's proposal is vulnerable to several objections. One is that tyranny can be produced through omission as well as commission. Threats of a veto could prevent measures from passing that would relieve ongoing tyranny, while the effort to avoid anarchy could motivate acquiescence in an unjust status quo.[22] The sacrifice of political equality should be obvious from the fact that groups of inevitably different sizes have the same veto. In this respect, the violation of political equality is like the one involved in districts of different populations having the same representation. Once again, we can see how difficult it is to fulfill all three of our conditions—political equality, nontyranny, and deliberation.

While Mill and Calhoun were willing to sacrifice political equality to deliberation (and perhaps nontyranny), we will see that American democracy has been moving in the general direction of sacrificing deliberation to (at least formal) political equality. It is very difficult to achieve all three of our core values. In the next chapter, I will outline a scheme for classifying democratic systems and then speculate on which positions in this scheme might permit the simultaneous realization of all three of our core values.

One caution: these three values are proposed as necessary conditions for a fully adequate realization of democracy in the large-scale nation-state, viewing the political system as a whole. Although democratic criteria are often applied to particular institutions and to subunits within the nation-state, the ultimate aim of this analysis is to determine whether an entire political system has achieved an adequate form of democracy. This aim is wholly compatible with granting that a particular institution—for example, the judiciary—may be largely or entirely immune from the considerations that would motivate efforts to apply all three of our proposed conditions to a particular institution. Yet the judiciary can play an essential role in assisting in the achievement of all three values in other institutions of the system. In the United States, for example, it is only through the courts that we have come closer to formal political equality;[23] the courts play a major role in restraining tyrannous possibilities;[24] they also add deliberation to the system independently of their effects on the structure of other institutions.[25] Our ultimate interest, however, is less in particular institutions than in the achievement of all three values in the system as a whole. For such an ambitious aim, clearly a new strategy is needed.

The Forms of Democracy
A Scheme

 Figure 1 pictures three dimensions or axes useful in describing and classifying democratic systems of government:

1. The north-south dimension can be thought of as Madisonian versus majoritarian democracy. By majoritarian I mean the degree to which majorities get their way, and by Madisonian I mean the degree to which there are impediments to majorities getting their way— impediments that are usually motivated by efforts to prevent tyranny of the majority. As Robert Dahl noted in his *Preface to Democratic Theory*, majority rule can be invoked as a guiding principle in a system, such as the American one, in which the operative decision-rule is actually "minorities rule." Intense minorities tend to get their way on issues of greatest concern to them. While this pattern is clearest in the United States, it occurs to some considerable degree elsewhere as well. Hence, it becomes an interesting empirical issue how, precisely, to place a given system on the north-south dimension.[1]

2. The east-west dimension can be thought of as representative versus direct democracy. It expresses the degree to which a mass public has the opportunity to participate in decision making directly, or the degree to which selected officials act on their behalf. The selection of political leaders will also vary in degree along this dimension. The change in the United States from indirect election (via state legislatures) to direct election of senators was a notable move to the west along this dimension. A similar point can be made about the proliferation of direct primaries in the presidential nomination system.

Figure 1

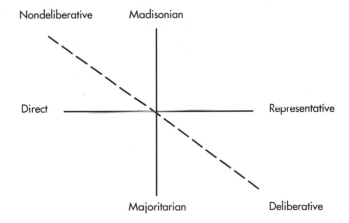

3. The near-far dimension can be thought of as deliberative versus nondeliberative democracy with respect to the
decision-making arena considered.

Figure 1 thus presents us with eight general categories within
which we can classify possibilities. The two-dimensional space
gives us four quadrants, and then the near-far dimension doubles
that. Our basic objective is to achieve near (deliberative) classifi-
cation for an institution that also managed, in its use of either
direct or representative institutions and in its placement on the
Madisonian-majoritarian dimension, to achieve both political
equality and nontyranny. The problem is to see if some version
of democratic institutions might fulfill all three conditions simultaneously. In pursuing this quest, we should not take figure
1 too literally. It is just a simplifying device for keeping track of a
number of possibilities and for sorting how these possibilities
might map into certain combinations of values.

Let us begin with the four quadrants of the two-dimensional
space and examine, in each case, the prospects for achieving a
deliberative (near) rather than nondeliberative (far) classifica-
tion.

Northeast quadrant. In this quadrant we can classify systems
and institutions that are representative and that also offer sig-

nificant impediments to majorities getting their way. Representative institutions may achieve both impediments to majority tyranny and opportunities for greater deliberation. As Madison argued in *Federalist* no. 10, the "delegation of the government" may serve "to refine and enlarge the public views by passing them through the medium of a chosen body of citizens, whose wisdom may best discern the true interest of their country and whose patriotism and love of justice will be least likely to sacrifice it to temporary or partial considerations." Madison speculates that the deliberations of such political leaders may represent a higher kind of democracy—not what the people happen to think given their passions and lack of information, but "the public voice" in some more thoughtful sense: "It may well happen that the public voice, pronounced by the representatives of the people, will be more consonant to the public good than if pronounced by the people themselves, convened for the purpose."[2]

Madison's problem of constitutional design was, in large part, to define the conditions under which an extended republic would produce circumstances "favorable to the election of proper guardians of the public weal,"[3] that is, representatives who would achieve this kind of deliberative consideration of the public good. Similarly, the famous argument in *Federalist* no. 10 was designed to show how impediments to majorities could prevent tyranny.[4]

The American political system generally fits into this northeast quadrant. Within this quadrant, we fall short of realizing all three values. Although we get some deliberation among political elites in representative institutions, and although there are a number of impediments to tyrannous policy choices, our realization of political equality is grossly defective. The improvements we have achieved in formal political equality do not prevent our structure of campaign financing from undermining political equality and denying an effective hearing to competing political viewpoints. As Judge J. Skelley Wright concludes: "Concentrated wealth, often channeled through political action committees, threatens to distort political campaigns and referenda. The voices of individual citizens are being drowned out in election campaigns—the forum for the political deliberations of our people. If the ideal of equality is trampled there, the principle of 'one person, one vote,' the cornerstone of our democracy, becomes a hollow mockery."[5]

It is a commonplace of political analysis that the United States does not have effective political equality because of the operation of PACs, the campaign finance system, and the role of organized interests. However, it is still an open question whether some possible institutions in the northeast quadrant, unlike our present ones, might actually achieve effective political equality. If such institutions preserved deliberation and non-tyranny, then our basic problem would have been solved. We will return to this possibility later.

Southeast quadrant. Here we have representative institutions that are more subject to majoritarian control. We can illustrate this by thinking about what seems to have happened to the U.S. Congress over the last few decades as the plebiscitary model of democracy has moved our institutions informally in the southern direction even when they cannot formally be moved too far to the southwest (and still remain representative institutions). In a plebiscitary model, political actors tend to behave with reference to what might win a plebiscite or popular referendum. The constant stream of opinion polls from competing sources is an important influence. The "electoral connection" and various new technologies (including the threat of attack videos) have made congressmen very sensitive to every variation in public opinion. The activities that David Mayhew described in *Congress: The Electoral Connection*—activities such as advertising, credit claiming, position taking—can all be rationalized within a plebiscitary model of political leadership. The rise of "outside" lobbying described by Gary Jacobson—lobbyists who threaten to mobilize at the grass-roots level, as opposed to the old "inside" lobbyists described by Raymond Bauer, Ithiel de Sola Pool, and Lewis Anthony Dexter—also fits a more plebiscitary model.[6] Given the vagaries of knowledge and deliberation among the mass electorate, the plebiscitary model of leadership seems to represent a comparative loss of deliberation.

The amalgamation of lobbying with public relations has facilitated (and been facilitated by) the spread of the plebiscitary model of leadership and representation. The small Washington lobbying firms have been acquired by massive public relations firms who bring to the lobbying process great expertise in manipulating the press and, via the press, public opinion. As Robert K. Gray, head of Hill and Knowlton's public affairs operation, explained to the *New York Times*, "We fill the Congressional mailbags by taking the story to the public and getting them to react back to the members. And then we can get to the members to lobby. If you accept the premise that in this country the power is with the people and the free press moves the people, this is a logical conclusion."[7]

What has happened to the Congress illustrates to a modest degree the general point of movement south in our diagram. A much more extreme example can be found in the history of the Electoral College—an institution that was originally supposed to be a deliberative body but now, when the electors are presumed to have no independence whatsoever, is an almost perfect relayer of (state-by-state) election returns.

The presidency is another institution that has undergone massive informal change in the direct-majoritarian direction. Presidential selection has moved southwest with the proliferation of direct primaries. But the presidency itself has also moved in the direction of majoritarian, popular control. What Jeffrey K. Tulis calls the modern "rhetorical presidency" contrasts sharply with the view of the Founders, for whom the presidency "was intended to be representative of the people, but not merely responsive to popular will. Drawn from the people through an election (albeit an indirect one), the president was to be free enough from the daily shifts in public opinion so that he could refine it, and paradoxically, better serve popular interests."[8]

With the rise of the "plebiscitary" and "rhetorical" presidency of the twentieth century, presidents began to speak directly to the people on important matters, instead of communicating their views in writing to Congress. Shorn of nineteenth-century inhibitions about the propriety of taking part in explicit policy debates, modern presidents commonly engage in "leadership through capsulization . . . the New Freedom, the New Deal, the Fair Deal, the Great Society, the New Federalism, Whip Inflation Now."[9] Popular discourse requires the simplified packaging that is effective with a mass audience. The presidency, as much as Congress, has moved, through *informal* constitutional and institutional change, in the plebiscitary direction of increased direct-majoritarianism. This movement is captured by Woodrow Wilson's memorable phrase that in the new system "public opinion must be truckled to . . . as is the majority so ought the government to be."[10]

Politicians have increasingly turned to pollsters for support and advice, from Franklin Roosevelt's reliance on the Princeton psychologist Hadley Cantril, to John Kennedy's on Louis Harris, to Lyndon Johnson's on Oliver Quayle and "Tad" Cantril,[11] to Jimmy Carter's on Pat Caddell.[12] With the Bush presidency, we have reached the point where a secretary of state, when questioned about the merits of his foreign policy, cites favorable poll results.[13] Some have even charged that President Bush only began to emphasize the supposedly "new urgency" of a possible Iraqi nuclear threat after poll results in the *New York Times* showed that this danger was far more effective in justifying American intervention in the Persian Gulf than any other argument.[14]

Applied to the presidency, the plebiscitary model is supported by what Sidney Blumenthal has called the "permanent campaign"[15]—a continuing sensitivity to public reception where "for the Reagan White House, every night is election night on television."[16] Blumenthal cites his interview with James Baker as White House chief of staff under Reagan to show that the distinction between campaigning and governing has broken down. "Politics and government are inseparable," Baker told him. "Polling is important to know the politics of a decision. And politics is inseparable from technique. . . . Campaign experience is good experience for a job like this. . . . Some of the things you do here are the same things you do in a campaign. You look to show off your president to best advantage. You capitalize on popularity by use of the same techniques as campaigning. It's not phony in any way."[17]

As Samuel Kernell argues, this continuing responsiveness to public opinion requires a simplification of political discourse suited to the mass publics whose opinions must be influenced and whose reactions must be anticipated. "As governing becomes campaigning, policy serves rhetoric," he writes. Actions are calculated in terms of their effect on public opinion and how they can be best presented to favorably influence public opinion. "Rather than the substance of detailed scrutiny and negotiations," Kernell concludes, "policy questions become oversimplified and stylized to satisfy the cognitive requirements of a largely inattentive national audience."[18]

Such simplifications, once accepted, can prove a trap. Bush struggled with the implications of his campaign slogan: "Read my lips; no new taxes." Later, frustrated by the need to remain flexible in interpreting this simple commitment, he offered a revision to reporters while jogging. "Read my lips" became "Read my hips."[19]

Once the president is motivated to respond to public opinion, he naturally attempts to manipulate it. To offer leadership he must seek "oratory to move an entire nation," as the *Washington Post* described Carter's task before his "crisis of confidence" speech.[20] Even Reagan's critics had to grant that he was a "great communicator." But for a president even to attempt to communicate directly to the people is a relatively recent phenomenon and a symptom of our general movement southwest in figure 1, toward a direct-majoritarian, plebiscitary model of leadership. "Prior to this century, presidents preferred written communications between the branches of government to oral addresses to 'the people,'" Tulis tells us. "The relatively few popular speeches that were made differed in character from today's addresses." Except for issues of war and peace, presidential speeches were generally limited to patriotic themes or major constitutional issues addressed in a nonpartisan way. Direct discourse on policy issues was exceedingly rare for nineteenth-century presidents.[21]

Since then, the combination of television, polling, and campaign reforms has created what Theodore Lowi,[22] James Ceaser,[23] and others have called the "plebiscitary president"—one whose success is constantly monitored in opinion polls, and for whom the management of public opinion and hence media images is all-important. "The desperate search," Lowi concludes, "is for the most effective presentation of appearances. This is a pathology because it escalates the rhetoric at home, ratcheting expectations upward notch by notch, and fuels adventurism abroad, in a world where the cost of failure can be annihilation."[24]

Northwest quadrant. The extreme northwest position can be distinguished from the extreme southwest position. We might imagine the Warner-Amex Qube system (a two-way cable television system set up for voting in the home) with majority rule as an example of the extreme southwest position. But the same system combined with Robert Paul Wolff's notion of *unanimous* direct democracy would fall into the northwest quadrant.[25] This is clearly a crazy proposal because it would give everyone a veto. Any person who wanted to block a new policy could do so. Although this system provides a perfect guarantee against tyranny by *commission,* it does nothing to protect against tyranny by *omission.* The point of mentioning the theoretical possibility of unanimous direct democracy is that it shows how the extreme Madisonian and extreme majoritarian positions are equally compatible with completely direct forms of democracy. The north-south and east-west axes in figure 1 are conceptually independent.

I argued in *Tyranny and Legitimacy* that tyranny was equally possible through omission as through commission. The unanimity rule takes the Madisonian impulse of providing impediments to new policies so far that it is counterproductive in preventing tyranny. We have only to imagine that severe deprivations will be imposed by a third party unless the government intervenes, or that a natural disaster creates a need for emergency relief (and irate taxpayers elsewhere want to veto the relief effort on grounds of cost), to see how severe deprivations that are avoidable might be imposed through omission.[26]

Whether or not the unanimous teledemocracy of Wolff's proposal would hold the public attention so as to be deliberative is another issue. Regardless, provided that severe deprivations can come about through omissions, such a system would not reliably avoid tyranny.

Southwest quadrant. Here is the explicit and, I believe, chimerical goal of a great deal of recent reforms. We should distinguish large-scale direct democracy from small-scale direct democracy. We tend to idealize the small-scale case as an example of the deliberative attractions of face-to-face democracy. Perhaps it once had some of these characteristics (setting aside the obvious omissions of slaves, women, and metics in the Athens of its origins). But the Federalists argued that small-scale direct democracy was *more* vulnerable to tyranny because it was more vulnerable to demagoguery. If they were right, even the small-scale version would likely fail at least one of our criteria.

In *Federalist* no. 63, Madison argues that direct democracy is vulnerable to tyranny in a way that representative institutions in a large-scale nation-state would not be. For example, he writes of the Senate:

> Such an institution may be sometimes necessary as a defence to the people against their own temporary errors and delusions. As the cool and deliberate sense of the community ought, in all governments and actually will, in all free governments, ultimately prevail over the views of its rulers; so there are particular moments in public affairs when the people, stimulated by some irregular passion, or some illicit advantage, or misled by the artful misrepresentations of interested men, may call for measures which they themselves will afterwards be the most ready to lament and condemn. In these critical moments, how salutary will be the interference of some temperate and respectable body of citizens, in order to check the misguided

career and to suspend the blow mediated by the people against themselves, until reason, justice and truth can regain their authority over the public mind? What bitter anguish would not the people of Athens have often escaped if their government had contained so provident a safeguard against the tyranny of their own passions? Popular liberty might then have escaped the indelible reproach of decreeing to the same citizens the hemlock on one day and statues on the next.[27]

It is worth noting that some forms of direct democracy may include protections against tyranny of the majority, protections of a kind that can be adopted in a small-scale, face-to-face society, but that are not possible in a large-scale nation-state. Consider, for example, the practices of a Quaker meeting where no votes are taken and where the discussion continues until a mutually recognized "sense of the meeting" emerges. "Patience, persuasion, the reformulation of questions so that they are acceptable to all, and a common conviction of the importance of a political system in which all are actually free and equal because no decisions are taken against anyone's will"—these are the characteristics and practices of a Quaker meeting (as described by Charles W. Anderson).[28] At the small scale, incorporating such practices into direct democracy safeguards against tyranny and promotes both political equality and deliberation. Such practices obviously raise decision-costs enormously. They are also a practical possibility only at the small scale, in what I am calling a face-to-face society.

At the large scale, we require some other strategy for achieving nontyranny and deliberation. As we have seen, Madison speculated that the very conditions defining an "extended republic" may offer protections against the nondeliberative and possibly tyrannous passions. "It may be suggested that a people spread over an extensive region," he wrote in *Federalist* no. 63, "cannot, like the crowded inhabitants of a small district, be subject to the infection of violent passions or to the danger of combining in pursuit of unjust measures."[29]

However, it is important to distinguish the small-scale from the large-scale version of direct democracy. It might be argued that the small-scale version achieves deliberation, at least on occasion, but at the cost of vulnerability to tyranny (apart from the special norms of a Quaker meeting). By contrast, we will see that the movement southwest in figure 1, when it is attempted at the scale of the large nation-state, carries with it a great lessening of deliberation. An extended republic, when it is representative and Madisonian, may serve nontyrannous deliberation. But an extended republic, when it is reformed in a southwestern direction to be made more direct, offers less prospect of serving either value.

Setting aside tyranny, one further value is at issue in the southwest quadrant. Thus far, we have discussed movement southwest as being motivated by political equality, but sometimes it is also advocated on the grounds of political participation, valued for its own sake. Participation is, in fact, one route to political equality, but, as we shall see, it is not the only route. To the extent that participation is valued independently of political equality, the only option for realization of that value is movement southwest.

Yet the primary reason for valuing participation, Carole Pateman argues, is its "educative" function, "educative in the very widest sense, including both the psychological aspect and the gaining of practice in democratic skills and procedures."[30] As Pateman points out, this argument works best in small-scale, face-to-face settings, particularly democracy in the workplace and in aspects of the local political environment that are close to home.

At the national level, the educative argument for participation confronts collective action problems—how to motivate individuals to acquire information for participation in the large-scale nation-state. As we shall see, the American experience with referendums and other variants of direct democracy does not support the view that by giving power to the people we also encourage educational efforts on their behalf to acquire the information to deliberate about the use of that power.

In what follows, I will assume that the basic trade-off of values posed by movement southwest versus movement northeast in figure 1 is a trade-off between political equality on the one hand and deliberation on the other. Movement southwest has been undertaken to serve political equality, while movement northeast serves deliberation.

Participation enters as a possible value in this debate because it is instrumental to political equality or, in its educative function, because it is instrumental to deliberation. If someone were to insist on the value of participation independent of its effect on *both* political equality and deliberation, then that advocate would be in the position of requiring even more movement in the southwestern direction. Since much of the burden of our argument here will be the significant costs in competing values of southwestern movement for the large-scale nation-state, I will not take further advocacy of participation for its own sake to be a tenable position. I will, rather, interpret our later task as one of overcoming the trade-offs posed by our diagram by envisioning new institutions that might achieve both political equality and deliberation. Participation will not be prized independently of these other values; it will, however, enter our discussions when it bears on either political equality or deliberation.

The March toward Direct Democracy

6 Alexis de Tocqueville saw an inevitable march toward the realization of "democracy" throughout the world: "Everywhere the various occurrences of national existence have turned to the advantage of Democracy: all men have aided it by their exertions. Those who have intentionally labored in its cause, and those who have served it unwittingly; those who have fought for it, and those who have declared themselves its opponents,—have all been driven along in the same track; have all labored to one end, some ignorantly, and some unwillingly."[1]

By democracy, Tocqueville meant a condition of social equality. The irony is that much of United States and indeed world history since he wrote would bear out his argument for the progress of democracy in the more narrow sense in which we currently apply it to political institutions. More specifically, the march of change has been in the general southwestern direction of figure 1—the direction of increasingly direct-majoritarian democracy.

In the United States, much of the history of amendments to the Constitution can be told as a story of increasing movement in this direction.[2] The amendments extend or help guarantee votes for women, blacks, residents of the nation's capital, and they provide for direct election of U.S. senators or for a lowered voting age. Other legal changes provide for one person one vote (preventing vote dilution) or, at the state level, for direct primaries and referendums.

Ironically, however, this long-term opening up of the system to mass participation has been accompanied by a massive decline in voter turnout. Great increases in the formal opportunities for direct-majoritarian control have been accompanied by massive nonparticipation and disinterest. It is worth noting that Switzerland, the other country that has most notably created opportunities for mass participation and direct democracy, also experiences extraordinarily low voter turnout. The United States ranks twentieth out of twenty-one major democracies in one international comparison; Switzerland ranks twenty-first.

Turnout in American elections is very low, viewed both comparatively and historically. As Walter Dean Burnham concludes in a recent paper, "Today, the USA has incomparably the lowest voting participation to be found in any advanced capitalist democracy with a policy-significant national government. Nationwide, 51.8% of adult citizen population voted for president in 1988. This is nearly 25% lower than the modal turnout in the United Kingdom or Canada, 35% lower than in much of continental Europe, and 40% lower than in countries like Sweden, Italy and Austria." One hundred years ago, turnout in American presidential elections may have approached 90 percent. Earlier turnout levels are even more impressive when one considers that American society was less educated and more rural one hundred years ago.[3] The current low levels are part of a long-term secular decline in turnout of great proportions, a secular decline which resists methodological criticisms.[4]

Yet the counterargument has sometimes been offered that if one considers turnout not among all of those eligible to vote, but among those who are actually registered to vote, the American record is not that bad. David Glass, Peveril Squire, and Raymond Wolfinger calculate that if one considers turnout as a percentage of *registered* voters, the United States jumps from 52.6 percent in 1980 (ranked twentieth out of twenty-one countries considered) to 86.8 percent (ranked eleventh). As a percentage of registered voters, this rate surpasses those of France, Denmark, the United Kingdom, and other countries in which a much higher percentage of the voting-age population actually goes to the polls.

The difference, of course, is that "the United States is the only country where the entire burden of registration falls on the individual rather than on the government."[5] A maze of state and local requirements and deadlines impedes those who are not truly interested in registering. American states that permit registration on election day have much higher turnout rates (for example, 67.2 percent in Wisconsin and 70.1 percent in Minnesota in 1980). Yet these rates still fall far short of the turnout in most of the other advanced countries. As a percentage of voting-age population, if the Wisconsin rate were somehow magically achieved by the entire United States,[6] it would move us up only to seventeenth place—still behind Spain (73 percent), Japan (74.4 percent), and the United Kingdom (76 percent), as well as such turnout leaders as Italy (94 percent) and Austria (89.3 percent).

Glass, Squire, and Wolfinger argue against the popular theory that "alienation" is an explanation for the gap between the United States and other countries. They point out that Americans do not rank markedly lower in survey questions about whether they are proud of their political institutions or are satisfied with the way democracy works in their country.[7]

Depending on what one means by alienation, it would certainly seem wide of the mark as an explanation. The recent history of angry voters, "outsider" candidate appeals, and anti-incumbency sentiments shows graphically that alienation may well contribute to participation rather than explain nonparticipation.

Arthur Hadley, in The Empty Polling Booth, painted a different picture of disconnection from the system by nonvoters. The major groups of nonvoters are not alienated so much as disconnected from politics. For example, 35 percent of the nonvoters in his study were "positive apathetics" who were absorbed with their personal lives but simply uninvolved in politics. He describes them as "happy, educated, well-off, but apathetic." They are more trusting of the government than the population as a whole (40 percent believe the government can be trusted to do the right thing most or all of the time, compared to just 36 percent of the general population). They are just too absorbed in their own lives to worry much about politics. Twenty-two percent comprise a group of the "politically impotent," whom Hadley characterizes as believing in luck or fate rather than political efficacy. Another group, the "bypassed" (13 percent), "are not highly cynical about government, not because they have not been turned off by politics but because they have no political awareness at all." Another 18 percent are prevented from voting for reasons beyond their control (because they moved too recently to register or have physical ailments).[8]

The picture that emerges of nonvoters is one of *disconnection* with politics. Nonvoters are preoccupied with their own lives, whether because they are happy (positive apathetics) or unhappy with them (the bypassed). Those with strong negative feelings are also said to trust to fate or luck, making political activity less appealing. All of this is compatible with a view of the American electorate as not being dramatically less proud of its institutions than counterparts in Western Europe. It is, nevertheless, a picture of an electorate with a massive portion of uninvolved citizens whose lives have very little connection with politics. We have created a system that permits participation but has failed to motivate it effectively.

Wolfinger and Steven Rosenstone have argued, in effect, that nonvoting does not really matter. Although they show that voters are "not a microcosm" but a "distorted sample" skewed along lines of education, class, race, age, ethnicity, and region, voters do not differ significantly from the entire electorate on current political issues. Apart from a slight gain for the Republicans of 3.7 percent compared to the general population, "voters are virtually a carbon copy of the citizen population. Those most likely to be underrepresented are those who lack opinions."[9]

Hence, in view of the issues that tend to be raised in the current system, it may not matter that so few people vote. Nonvoters, while differing significantly in education, class, and other areas, do not now have different opinions on the issues the system has on its current agenda. Should we then assume that our massive levels of nonparticipation are not cause for concern? Those levels should be interpreted, first, as a symptom of disconnection from the political system on the part of the half of the electorate that does not participate in presidential elections, and on the part of the nearly two-thirds of the electorate that does not participate in many other elections. Second, those levels of nonparticipation invite us to engage in the thought-experiment: What issues might be raised by the system if it more effectively realized the core values of democracy we have emphasized, particularly deliberation and political equality? Innovations of the kind I will discuss in the final chapter are designed to give the interests of all strata of society a more effective hearing and to infuse deliberation into institutions that also embody political equality. Such innovations would change the evolution of issues, the emergence of candidates, the articulation of interests. The fact that our present quiescent, disengaged public has not bothered to think enough about politics to have public opinions (rather than political preferences) worthy of the name, does not mean that it might not arrive at more informed and more deliberative opinions under conditions designed to truly engage it. Bringing the massive, quiescent portions of the electorate into our public political dialogue might well make a difference. Whether it would or not cannot be predicted from the lack of difference between voters and nonvoters under present conditions, when neither group is deeply engaged or deliberative in its political thinking and participation.

Similar points may be made about the public reaction to the proliferating opportunities to vote in referendums. The number of referendums on the ballot has increased extraordinarily, particularly in the western states. In 1990, there were at least sixty-seven proposals on statewide ballots, the largest number since 1932.[10] Yet referendums are vulnerable to mass disinterest (so that little deliberation is achieved) and to distortions from grossly unequal funding (undermining political equality). "Local referendums often attract less than five per cent of registered voters to the polls."[11] The *Dallas Morning News* notes that "in some cases turnout is even lower. In April 1978 only 7,042 people—2.1 percent of Dallas' registered voters—participated in a special election to consolidate [Dallas] with the city of Kleberg."[12]

Referendums need not be very deliberative. David O. Sears and Jack Citrin studied Proposition 13 (the tax revolt in California) and identified "a surge of recklessness, a period of nearly blind emotion, surrounding the passage of Proposition 13, when anger at government seemed to dominate the public's thinking. The usual explanations for the voters' choices still held sway, but this added hostility proved a potent weapon for the tax revolt. At that point, the tide of anti-government emotions eroded stable attitudes about what government should do. The public's desire for maintaining the status quo of services plummeted, their perceptions of governmental inefficiency rose considerably, and their anger focused on the 'bureaucrats.'"[13]

A similar description could be applied to the forces that led to the 1990 passage of term limitations for state legislators in California, Oklahoma, and Colorado. Twenty other states have had proposals introduced at the time of this writing. To see how referendums move the system in the majoritarian, anti-Madisonian direction, imagine how the prospects for term limitations at the national level would change if the referendum mechanism were available nationally. A Gallup poll before the 1990 elections put nationwide support for term limits for Congress at 73 percent.[14] Without the referendum mechanism, political elites can frustrate the passions that direct-majoritarianism would voice, providing time for deliberation and debate.

Such experiences with direct referendums illustrate the dangers of direct democracy noted by Madison. As we saw earlier, he warned that "the people, stimulated by some irregular passion, or some illicit advantage, or misled by the artful misrepresentations of interested men, may call for measures which they themselves will afterwards be the most ready to lament and condemn."

There are also real issues to be raised about the extent to which mass primaries have succeeded in achieving political equality. Turnout runs about half the already low levels for general elections, and it is disproportionately weighted toward the wealthier and more educated voters. Even with formal political equality, this pattern brings into question the extent to which the interests of all strata of society are getting an effective hearing in the process. Hence, the account of direct democracy may be altogether too optimistic, even on its chosen ground of political equality.

The most striking area of reform in the southwestern direction has been in American presidential nominations. The McGovern-Fraser Commission, spawned by the turbulence of the 1968 Democratic presidential convention, articulated the effort to bring power to the people. "The cure for the ills of democracy," it announced, was "more democracy." The two principles enunciated by the commission were "participation" and "popular control."[15]

Nelson Polsby aptly summarizes the overall change. He characterizes the reforms since 1968 "as parts of an underlying transformation of the nomination process from an elite to a mass phenomenon. Advocates of this transformation have appealed to the neutral principle of political equality: far more people now participate in the process than was true before 1968. This has been accomplished, however, at the cost of deliberation."[16]

It might be argued that a certain social cohesion or political community within the party would be necessary for its institutions to serve any process of deliberation. If so, the proliferation of primaries has undermined that social cohesion. Even if some neoconservative critics of the party reforms overstate the character of that social cohesion, they make a point in concluding, like Jeanne Kirkpatrick, that "the capacity to appeal directly to voters makes it possible to bypass not only the party leadership, but the dominant political class, their standards and their preferences." She argues, more generally:

It is almost impossible to overstate the impact of primaries on the nominating process. They affect the character of delegates, candidates, campaigns, conventions and parties. Convention delegates chosen in presidential primaries are selected because of their relationship to a presidential candidate instead of their relationship to the party. Since a national convention is the highest decision-making body for a party, choosing delegates without regard to their knowledge of or commitment to the party means vesting control over a party in persons who may have little concern for it. That is not all. Because candidates can go directly to the voters in search of the nomination, primaries permit candidates as well as delegates to be selected without having ever served an apprenticeship in the party, without ever being screened in or socialized by the party.[17]

While it is certainly true that primaries have made it far easier for candidates to evade "peer review" by other politicians and by whatever might be taken to constitute the "political class," it might be argued that it has not mattered very much for quite awhile who attends the national conventions. There has not been a multiballot convention on the Democratic side since 1952 and on the Republican side since 1948. The decline of conventions as deliberative bodies occurred long before the proliferation of primaries and may be taken, in itself, as another part of the movement toward a plebiscitary model of democracy. Conventions have become scripted television events where the delegates cannot even introduce resolutions. If the purpose were to decide the nominee, they could be held by mail. The purpose is now to launch the media-based television candidacies of the party nominees in the general election.[18]

The reforms, coupled with new technologies, have moved candidates to rely on their own independent organizations rather than on party organizations. Television, polling, direct mail solicitation, and the federalization of campaign financing have all increased the independence of candidates from state party organizations that used to perform the functions of connecting candidates to voters, providing information about public opinion, raising money, and providing access to big contributors. Rather than relying on state parties and their leaders, candidates have every incentive now to rely on their own independent organizations.[19]

The proliferation of primaries increases the reliance on television by both candidates and voters, not only in the primaries, but in the ever more demanding process of raising funds required to compete in them. The primaries are far more expensive than caucuses or state party conventions. Campaign finance reforms have meant that candidates must turn to direct mail to raise the necessary funds. And direct mail favors those with already established visibility: "Anonymous givers by mail are far more likely to send money to candidates of whom they have heard."[20]

In 1968 in the Democratic party, seventeen primaries selected 48.7 percent of the delegates; in 1988, thirty-seven primaries selected 81.4 percent of the delegates. On the Republican side there has been a similar transformation, from seventeen primaries selecting 47 percent of the delegates to thirty-eight primaries selecting 80.7 percent of the delegates.[21]

At the state level, the spread of the primary was consolidated in the 1920s as the result of the first wave of enthusiasm for progressive reforms. Writing in 1941, a biographer of Robert La Follette could assess the success of the primary idea at the state level by noting that in 1940, "forty-four states held direct primaries; in a majority of these states the nomination of all state officers, United States senators, and congressmen by this method is mandatory." The spread of the primary idea at the state level, Allen Lovejoy noted, was facilitated by the one-party character of many state political systems.[22]

The parallel and more recent proliferation of presidential primaries constitutes a movement of the selection system in a southwestern direction, but at the eventual cost of decreasing deliberation. As Kiku Adato showed in a striking recent study comparing television newscasts on all three major networks in 1968 and 1988: "The average sound bite or bloc of uninterrupted speech fell from 42.3 seconds for presidential candidates in 1968 to only 9.8 seconds in 1988. In 1968 almost half of all sound bites were 40 seconds or more, compared to less than one percent in 1988. In fact, it was not uncommon in 1968 for candidates to speak, uninterrupted, for over a minute on the evening news (21 per cent of sound bites); in 1988 it never happened."[23]

Now if a candidate can't say it in under ten seconds, it does not have much chance of getting on the evening news. (The last sentence takes about seven seconds to speak, so you can see how short a period we are discussing.) Paul Brountas, Michael Dukakis's campaign chairman, was told by a television reporter during the 1988 campaign, "Goddamn it, Paul. You've got to get your candidate to stop pausing between sentences. He's taking 22 seconds to complete a thought."[24] Bits of political discourse on television have been reduced to what Bill Moyers has called "fortune cookies."[25]

As Bruce Buchanan showed in his recent Markle Commission report, the media devoted almost 60 percent of their 1988 campaign coverage to the political horse race and to candidate conflicts, and only about 30 percent to issues and candidate qualifications.[26] In a similar vein, I calculate from the work of Michael Robinson and Margaret Sheehan that if you took the entire preconvention period from January to June 1980, CBS offered a total of 450 minutes of campaign coverage, of which 307.8 minutes were classified by Robinson and Sheehan as horse race coverage. Hence, only a bit more than two of the seven and one-half hours were devoted to coverage of either candidates or issues.[27] These totals cover all the primaries and must be divided among all the candidates. Even on issues to which the media devote a lot of attention, there is evidence that it is hard to get through. According to Buchanan's study, just after Labor Day in 1988, despite extensive media coverage after the conventions, 34 percent of the electorate did not know who vice presidential candidate Dan Quayle was, and 53 percent were unable to identify Lloyd Bentsen. An earlier, equally disheartening commentary on mass publics: "In 1964, 62 percent of the American public did not know that the Soviet Union was not in NATO."[28] As Luskin concludes a systematic review of the evidence on political sophistication, "The distributional evidence is clear: by anything approaching elite standards, the American public is extremely unsophisticated about politics and has not become appreciably more so over the past two and a half decades." He adds that "other publics, abroad, are similarly unsophisticated."[29]

Hence, it seems reasonable to conclude that while movement in the southwestern direction may bring power to the people, it is unlikely to bring thoughtful or deliberative power to the people. The main proposals offered in response to the limitations of southwestern reforms have been an effort to move back northeast. But such efforts will strike mass publics as undemocratic because they would undermine political equality. Clearly, strategies of democratic reform have been caught in a dilemma, a forced choice between political equality and deliberation. My proposal of deliberative opinion polls is one way of dealing with this dilemma. In part 3 we will see that there are other possibilities as well.

Part Three
Prospects for Democracy

Politico-Economic Systems
The Problem of Democratic Transitions

7 My diagnosis of the difficulties facing democratic reform in the United States has centered on the claim that only a direct-majoritarian vision of democracy is considered legitimate in the public eye. This vision, represented by the southwest quadrant in figure 1, has such a hold over the popular imagination that the values served by the other legitimate versions of democracy have been sacrificed. Viable democratic reform, I concluded, should focus on innovations that would fill out the northeast quadrant—innovations that would reformulate representative institutions so as to achicvc both political equality and deliberation.

As we look around the world, a similar conclusion emerges. The unique legitimacy attaching to direct-majoritarian democracy, whether in the form of referendums or of a "democracy of the streets," poses a major impediment to the transitions to democracy now being attempted in other countries. The risks that Mikhail Gorbachev ran in his March 1991 referendum on preserving the Soviet Union illustrate the dangers of the direct-majoritarian stranglehold on popular legitimacy. Unless representative institutions can be devised that offer legitimacy comparable to the direct-majoritarian voice of the people, transitions, particularly for those countries attempting the twofold movement to democracy and a market economy, have only dubious prospects of success. Innovations in representation, innovations in our northeast quadrant, may be crucial not only for improvements in democracy in the United States but also for transitions to democracy around the world.

We are in an unprecedented period of new democracies. Over the last two decades, at least thirty-two formerly authoritarian regimes have held relatively free and contested elections. How many of these states will be able to consolidate a lasting transition to democracy remains, however, an open question. The transformation of the Eastern bloc is, of course, the most striking new chain of events. Free elections returned to Poland in 1989 and to Czechoslovakia, Hungary, Romania, and Bulgaria in 1990. In Latin America, there were notable movements toward democracy in Peru (1980), Chile (1989), Argentina (1983), Uruguay (1984), and Brazil (1985). Other major transitions to relatively free elections have occurred in Spain (1977), Portugal (1976), Greece (1974), Turkey (1983), and South Korea (1988). There are many other important cases where the character of the elections is open to dispute or where special factors were present.[1] Nevertheless, these events add up to an extraordinary resurgence of democratic institutions.

Many of these actual or potential transitions to democracy also represent transformations of the entire politico-economic system. Hence, we need to consider, at least in a general way, the relations between politics and economics. The simple fourfold table (figure 2) summarizes the problem. If we consider politics on one dimension and economics on the other, we can come up with two simple classifications in each case: democratic and nondemocratic forms of organization for the state, market-oriented and nonmarket-oriented forms of organization for the economy. Of course, these classifications oversimplify many complex matters. They are matters of degree. There are significant elements of hierarchy, coercion, and indoctrination in every known market system, just as there are usually significant market elements within state socialist or planned economies. Democracy is also a complex matter of degree. Nevertheless, a line can reasonably be drawn between economic systems that rely primarily on market mechanisms and those that rely primarily on mechanisms of the state (coercion or indoctrination).[2] Similarly, political institutions can be divided into those that have a position on our three-dimensional scheme of democratic possibilities (at a minimum through competitive elections conducted without significant fraud or coercion to select a govern-

Figure 2

Economics

Politics	Market-oriented	Nonmarket
Democratic	1	2
Nondemocratic	4	3

ment) and those that do not. These distinctions account for the four possibilities pictured in figure 2.

Once we divide the world's politico-economic systems into the four basic theoretical possibilities pictured in this table, the great mystery emerges of why box 2 is virtually empty. A partial explanation relies on the historical contingency that the quests for political liberty and for certain economic liberties arose together.[3] However, such a contingent explanation leaves open the theoretical possibility that democratic political liberties and market-related economic liberties can be separated, as in those systems represented in box 4.

The contemporary problem of transitions to democracy must be seen in terms of movements either from box 4 to box 1 or from box 3 to box 1. Nicaragua is an especially controversial example of a country that attempted to move from box 3 to box 2. Chile tried to move to box 2 under Allende. When that effort collapsed, the country moved from box 2 to box 4, and is now moving from box 4 to box 1. The former state socialist systems of Eastern Europe are generally attempting to move from box 3 to box 1.

Successful and familiar transitions such as those of Spain, Greece, Portugal, and many Latin American cases fit a movement from box 4 to box 1. However, the collapse of the state socialist systems has created the virtually unprecedented problem of movement from box 3 to box 1. We must emphasize that the movement from box 4 to box 1 does not offer a road map for the very different problems of how to move from box 3 to box 1. For that twofold transition, many of the issues are unprecedented and we have few guideposts. While Gorbachev has, himself, invoked the example of King Juan Carlos of Spain (as a "kind of guarantor of political stability" in the Spanish transition to democracy), the two cases are not comparable. In the first place, the Soviet Union requires a far more massive economic transformation than Spain. In the second place, the king, as head of state but not chief executive, did not have to take direct, continuing responsibility for public policy as Gorbachev does.[4]

The bulk of this book explores what should go in box 1 once a political system gets there and how efforts to fill out box 1 might be improved. How to get there is a separate question, particularly when the starting point is a politico-economic system so different that we can highlight the difference by classifying it in a different box.

Many current issues can be placed within this admittedly simple framework. For example, the Soviet Union can be seen as grappling with the choice between moving from box 3 to box 1, or from box 3 to the largely uncharted territory of box 2. The first option is associated with Boris Yeltsin, the president of the Russian republic, the second with Nikolai Ryzhkov, the chairman of the Council of Ministers of the USSR from 1985 to 1990. As president of the Soviet Union, Gorbachev for a long time maintained an ambiguous position between the two options. In 1990 Ryzhkov accused him of leaving the Soviet economy "with neither a plan nor a market."[5]

Democratic socialists have long aspired to bring about a transition from box 1 to box 2. The dream of Eduard Bernstein has, however, proven an elusive goal.[6] In some interpretations, Marx himself offered a variant of our box 2 rather than the Leninist distortions of box 3.[7] But it should be noted that a democratic socialist transformation was frustrated in many societies by the nondirect, nonmajoritarian character of most democratic systems—a character which permitted them to frustrate what may well have been popular subscription to socialist ideals in many cases. "It must not be forgotten that in many democracies close to a majority of the population favored, in principle, a socialized economy," Juan Linz notes. "The democratic governments that did not socialize the means of production were indirectly protecting or legitimizing capitalist economic systems, sometimes more effectively than any authoritarian regime could. In doing so, in some cases they were bearing a cost for not realizing the will of the people." The fact that the form of democracy was not very far in the direct-majoritarian direction prevented the systems from being buffeted by any real attempts to move out of box 1. Now the situation has changed. The undermining of nonmarket alternatives provides a boost to those regimes which managed to maintain market systems, popular views to the contrary. The nonmarket alternatives, at least for the time being, have lost their popular legitimacy. "Indirectly," Linz concludes, "the crisis of full socialism contributes to the stability and legitimacy of democracies unwilling or unable to move toward socialism."[8] Furthermore, the current delegitimation of socialist economic structures renders the prospects for any movements from box 1 to box 2 unlikely in the near future.

For democratic socialism to come about through an electoral competition, Adam Przeworski and John Sprague note that class-based political parties would have to obtain a majority in competition with parties based on innumerable other loyalties, including "various particularistic claims made on behalf of confessional persuasions, ethnic ties, linguistic affinities, regional, racist or nationalistic values."[9] While many people who vote for these electoral competitors may have subscribed to socialism in principle, they did not subscribe to it intensely enough to support it in preference to these other loyalties. Left-based parties faced the dilemma of holding on to their bases among workers while still attracting enough of these other potential supporters to get a majority. Electoral strategies aimed at the former would undermine the latter and vice versa. None of them ever succeeded. And the class structure has since been changing so that the size of the base for socialist parties among workers has been shrinking. After a hundred years of electoral socialism, "left wing parties face a secular decline." With respect to the major parliamentary democracies, Przeworski and Sprague argue that "there is every indication that the proportion of workers in the labor force, in the population, and thus in the electorate, has begun to decrease at least after 1960 and is now falling at a precipitous rate, so rapidly that we now speak of 'deindustrialization.'" For this, among other reasons, they conclude that "the era of electoral socialism may be over."[10]

The great danger facing countries that try to make the transition from box 3 to box 1 is that, because box 3 systems do not have a market economy, their efforts to move to box 1 will involve so much economic dislocation that they may be undermined politically. For this reason, they face the possibility of challenges from authoritarian-market combinations which may forestall political democracy by using economic development as a means of legitimating themselves. In a way, this was the Pinochet solution in Chile.[11] Of course, the model of Chile is not directly applicable to Eastern Europe. To single out some obvious differences, Chile has great economic inequalities, a developed party system, and a history of military interventions in politics. The legacy of the state socialist systems has been a leveling of economic inequalities and an absence of political parties, a void now being filled by an overheated proliferation of new, undeveloped parties.[12] Despite these differences, I mention Chile to illustrate the general points that efforts to democratize may conceivably lead to box 4 (rather than boxes 1 or 2) and that such efforts may, for a time, yield impressive economic development. In some situations, an authoritarian-market system may mobilize resources for economic development better than a democratic system. Under such conditions, a population may be faced with the harsh choice between economic development without democracy and democracy without economic development. If the former really delivers the goods, then some regimes may find a working consensus on institutions that fall far short of even minimal democratic aspirations. The precise form of the authoritarian regime promoting economic development may still be an open question. It need not be the "bureaucratic authoritarianism" of Latin America.[13] The former state socialist systems of Eastern Europe may well produce their own varieties. The point is that box 4 is a worrisome alternative to the possibility of successful transitions to democracy in box 1. The perils of transforming the entire politico-economic system rather than just the political system, as in our standard cases of successful transition to democracy, remain to be explored.

We have preliminary indications from Eastern Europe of how tumultuous this twofold transition can be. Prime Minister Tadeusz Mazowiecki's third-place finish in Poland's presidential elections was widely attributed to his getting much of the blame for the economic dislocations caused by Poland's attempt to make a rapid transition to the market. In the first year, industrial output and wages dropped more than 20 percent. "When Czechoslovak officials decided to close a highly polluting, energy-inefficient, unprofitable aluminum plant in Slovakia," the *New York Times* noted, "a huge public protest persuaded the Government to give the factory a year's reprieve."[14] Hungary's privatization minister, Istvan Tompe, was dismissed after a strong public reaction to the low share price he demanded for the first state-owned company to be privatized. Giving away state assets provoked a public outcry, but Tompe's defenders countered that the flood of buyers attracted by the price created momentum and publicity for the entire program of privatization.

Elections are one thing; the task of maintaining continuing public support for a fragile regime is something else entirely. The Czech republic's economic minister, Karel Dyba, commented to a reporter: "People voted for a Government that promised hardships, lower living standards and some unemployment. It's one thing to be for a market economy, and another thing to experience the not-so-nice side of a market economy. . . . Nobody can tell what the tolerance limit of the public will be."[15]

Such examples show the difficulty of combining political accountability and market considerations.[16] Particularly when political accountability is both informal (including accountability to street demonstrations and perceptions of popular sentiment) and direct-majoritarian, the result can be a tumultuous reaction to economic dislocations. If and when fledgling democratic systems become more consolidated, there may be more of a chance for less direct, less majoritarian deflections of popular sentiment. Then political institutions might be in a better position to withstand the heat of popular demands. It is the difficulty of making the twofold transition from box 4 to box 1 that raises such unprecedented issues.

These difficulties raise the disturbing possibility that a system in uneasy transition from box 3 may move to box 4 rather than to box 1. Such a regime would offer its citizens (relative) prosperity rather than effective voting rights. Faced with the alternatives of economic development without democracy or democracy without economic development, it is quite possible that many citizens would choose the former.

We would be naively optimistic to think that the present flowering of democratic reforms can sustain itself without enough progress on the economic side to provide a basis for the legitimacy of the entire politico-economic system. Shevardnadze's chilling prophecy in his resignation speech symbolizes the threat hanging over efforts to move the Soviet Union from box 4. "Dictatorship is coming. I state it with complete responsibility," he warned. "No one knows of what kind this dictatorship will be, and who will come—what kind of dictator, what the regime will be like."[17]

It should be obvious that democracy does not ensure the success of an economy. Conversely, the failure of an economy does not ensure the failure of a democracy. A transition to democracy does not, by itself, imply a transition to a market system if one was lacking, nor does it imply a transition to a more successful market system if the previous one was less successful. That box 2 is virtually empty implies that markets may have become a necessary condition for democratic systems. But the relation between the political and economic dimensions is not well understood. Some have argued that it is due to mere historical contingency, rather than to any necessary relation, that no consolidated cases have emerged in box 2. It is also true that the recent experiment in Nicaragua can be thought of as an attempt to provide the kind of system that would fill out box 2. At this writing, however, it seems unlikely that this attempt will succeed.[18]

On the other hand, we should not assume that economic failure will, by itself, always knock a regime out of box 1 into one of the nondemocratic alternatives (boxes 3 or 4). Regimes may have consolidated a general commitment to democratic processes to the point that they can withstand prolonged economic crisis. Linz notes, for example: "The world depression that presumably destroyed the democracy in Weimar and Austria created more unemployment in Norway and in the Netherlands and in fact consolidated the Norwegian democracy. The Dutch government was one of the most long-lasting after the depression. The degree of institutional legitimacy was more decisive than the economic crisis."[19]

Yet the economic failures of an already consolidated democratic system must be distinguished from the more daunting problem of the economic failures of a regime in transition. The unprecedented challenge facing regimes in box 3 that are attempting to move to box 1 cannot be underestimated. In this connection, President Zhelyv Zhelev of Bulgaria has stated that his country is merely undergoing a transition from one form of capitalism to another, since the previous state socialist system was really a form of "state monopoly capitalism." The implication is that the transition to merely another form of capitalism should not be regarded as insuperable. Such statements can be taken as a symptom of the difficulties of moving from box 3 to box 1, as opposed to the better-known path of moving from box 4 to box 1.[20]

It is worth pausing to juxtapose figure 2 with the map of democratic possibilities in figure 1. Movement from either box 3 or 4 to box 1 must encounter the problem that if the version of democracy that has legitimacy is the simple direct-majoritarian one, then there is great room for the related dangers of lack of deliberation, radical instability, and tyranny of the majority (because of the prospects for inflaming whatever economic, racial, or ethnic divisions there may be in the society). The very notion of bringing "power to the people" implies a lack of what Americans would think of as Madisonian checks, an openness to inflamed, immediate passions, and a constant process of accountability, all of which may be difficult to maintain during a democratic transition. However difficult this may be in the case of a market-oriented system making the transition to democracy (box 4 to box 1), it is likely to be far more difficult and disruptive in the case of a nonmarket system making the transition from box 3 to box 1, because the economic dislocations for which the political system will be held accountable are likely to be far more profound than in a market-oriented economy. The full range of democratic possibilities I have asserted in the three-dimensional chart (figure 1) is worth emphasizing, because unless the less direct and less majoritarian forms of democracy maintain some legitimacy, many attempts to make the democratic transition may prove impossible.

On the other hand, we cannot assume that referendums and other forms of direct democracy will always be destabilizing. Agenda manipulation may permit leaders to determine which questions are asked in a referendum in such a way that actual majority opinion might be more frustrated under direct democracy than under representative forms of government. The spectacle of Estonian leaders *resisting* Gorbachev's call for a referendum on a new all-union treaty after their republican legislature had voted to secede from the Soviet Union shows their awareness of the danger of agenda manipulation and question framing. Most observers agree that there is overwhelming popular sentiment for secession in Estonia. Yet the call to secede comes from an elected legislature, and leaders there have resisted a referendum on Gorbachev's treaty directly affecting the same issue.[21]

Despite such exceptional cases, it is generally true that referendums and other forms of direct democracy are open to sudden bursts of popular enthusiasm that indirect forms of democracy are positioned to frustrate.

In this context, it is disturbing to realize that it is precisely the direct-majoritarian notion of democracy that has commonly been invoked in democratic transitions. It is the notion that has most immediate plausibility to mass publics. This legitimacy applies both to what might be termed formal or institutionalized versions of direct democracy, such as primaries and referendums, as well as to what might be termed informal direct democracy. By this I mean the invocation of imputed direct-majoritarian decisions based on some other indicator. The plebiscitary model of political leadership discussed earlier is one example; another, more tumultuous example is the use of street demonstrations to object to or bring down a government, rationalized as a form of direct democracy. This way of thinking about mass participation had some currency in the United States in the sixties.[22] Its danger for democratic transitions can be seen from recent events in Bulgaria, where mass demonstrations brought down a government that had won a majority in free elections. If one posits abiding by the results of a procedurally fair election as a necessary part of any consolidated transition to democracy, then the use of *informal* direct democracy (when it is not part of the agreed-on electoral system) to undermine the legitimacy of formal democratic results, produces an important new source of instability for transitions.[23]

Spain offers a case of a successful transition to democracy in a multicultural, multinational, and multilingual society. This transition was managed by certain crucial elites; the notion of democracy was not used to dismember the society. Manipulation of political agendas and choice of appropriate arenas of decision can make all the difference in determining whether a particular state survives democratization intact. In the Spanish case, the Basque minority, which clearly favored independence, was frustrated by a decision not to permit the autonomy issue to be voted on regionally until after national elections in 1977.[24] Without careful manipulation of the choice of arenas for decision and of the questions posed, prospects in many emergent democracies with regionally defined cleavages might be comparable to those of Yugoslavia. A common quip in Western Europe is that by the year 2000, there will be only seven states in Europe—a United States of Europe and the six republics of what was once Yugoslavia. This hypothetical scenario illustrates the point that democracy can be employed both to disaggregate and to aggregate states.

Plebiscites for independence in Slovenia and possibly Croatia illustrate that what is intended, at the elite level, as part of a negotiation for terms of confederation may be viewed by the masses as an assertion of a previously submerged national identity.[25] As the process of mass democratic expression acquires a dynamic of its own[26] and influences similar processes in neighboring republics,[27] a democratic decomposition of the entire state becomes more likely.[28]

The crucial issue in applying any sort of democratic decision-rule is, of course, to know the boundaries of the electorate that is entitled to take part in the decision. Amazingly little serious work in political theory has been done on this problem.[29] How open this issue is to manipulation can be seen from the Irish question. If one had a referendum in Northern Ireland, statistically dominated by the Protestants, one might well imagine support for its continuing status as part of the United Kingdom. Alternatively, if one had such a referendum in Ireland as a whole, the Catholic majority might well support the incorporation of Northern Ireland into the Republic. Finally, if a referendum were held throughout the British Isles on the status of Northern Ireland, one could easily imagine support for the position that Britain should retain Northern Ireland. Depending on the boundaries chosen, the result will differ.[30] One cannot use democratic decision-rules without some prior basis for determining the boundaries of the state within which they are to be applied.

When issues of secession combine with efforts to make the twofold transition from box 4 to box 1, the result is explosive.

Gorbachev reportedly refused to go along with the Shatalan plan for a market transition in five hundred days because it would have converted the Soviet Union into a loose confederation. Yeltsin stands, in these debates, not only for the market but for far greater autonomy for the Russian republic. As the economic dislocations continue, Ed Hewitt concludes in his survey of the Soviet economic situation, "republics and even cities will respond to the crisis by seeking to hold onto the scarce products they produce, increasing the fragmentation of the economy." This movement toward economic secession creates incentives for a similar movement toward political secession. "Republican leaders," Hewitt argues, "find it not only politically profitable but imperative to fight for their sovereignty in an attempt to abandon what appears to them to be a sinking ship."[31]

Sometimes the transition to democracy will even result in the disappearance of the state in question. East Germany, democratically incorporated into the new German state, is a case in point. Clearly, democracy can be employed to produce new states, to destroy old ones, to break up states, and to consolidate them. Normative democratic theory has not worked out which kind of question should be put to what construction of the people under what conditions. The ambiguities of "self-determination" are not, to any significant degree, resolved by international law. Self-determination requires some consensus for the "self" that is to do the determining (which is why the notion has found its uncontested applications in the liberation of former colonies).[32] Yet depending on how these decision problems are posed, a given state and people may or may not make the transition to democracy.

Empirically, the transition problem opens up uncharted territories. Guillermo O'Donnell and Philippe Schmitter compare the problem to the unpredictability of a multilayered chess game, but with the proviso that any number may be playing at the same time (and, we might add, that some of the rules may be revised as the players go along). The fate of democracy will depend on "the high degree of indeterminacy embedded in situations where unexpected events . . . , insufficient information, hurried and audacious choices, confusion about motives and interests, plasticity and even indefinition of political identities, as well as the talents of specific individuals . . . are frequently decisive in determining the outcomes."[33]

New Structures of Representation
Deliberative Opinion Polls and Other Proposals

8 The basic problem facing proponents of democratic reform is that movement southwest in figure 1, while it may further political equality, has tended to undermine deliberation. Conversely, movement northeast, while favoring deliberation (at least by political elites), has tended to undermine political equality. The central question remains: are there possible reforms that would serve both political equality and deliberation?

As I have already noted, we have only imperfectly adapted democracy to the large scale. The apparent conflict between political equality and deliberation may be avoidable if we are creative enough in reformulating the institutions of representation that fit into the northeast quadrant. *Conventional* representative institutions have sacrificed either political equality or deliberation. There may be other forms of representation that do not.

I believe there are several possible institutional innovations that might be employed to further both deliberation and political equality. Since there is no reason to believe they should increase the risk of tyranny,[1] such innovations can be credibly offered as contributions to a polity that might achieve all three of our core values.

Let us return to the notion of a deliberative opinion poll. An ordinary poll models what the electorate thinks, given how little it knows. A deliberative opinion poll models what the electorate *would* think if, hypothetically, it could be immersed in intensive deliberative processes. The point of a deliberative opinion poll is prescriptive, not predictive. It has a recommending force, telling us that this is what the entire mass public would think about some policy issues or some candidates if it could be given an opportunity for extensive reflection and access to information.

81

Returning to American politics, recall that the McGovern-Fraser Commission, which set off the proliferation of mass primaries in the United States, explicitly resisted proposals to supplant the Democratic party convention with a national primary on the grounds that a national convention offered an opportunity for face-to-face deliberation. But as we have seen, the national political conventions are no longer deliberative events. The very process of democratizing the selection of delegates has left the national conventions bound, mechanically, to preselected options determined by the results of the primaries. In terms of the core function of candidate selection, the national conventions are now not much more deliberative than the Electoral College—an institution whose original deliberative character was similarly tamed by direct-majoritarianism.

The same argument that the McGovern-Fraser Commission offered for retaining the national political conventions applies to my proposal for giving deliberative opinion polls a role in the process of selecting presidential candidates: "The face-to-face confrontation of Democrats of every persuasion in a periodic mass meeting is productive of healthy debate, important policy decisions (usually in the form of platform planks), reconciliation of differences, and realistic preparation for the fall presidential campaign."[2]

Of course, I am not proposing to limit deliberative opinion polls to any one party. As noted earlier, both parties can be represented in a single event. Or perhaps separate events could be mounted as a prelude to the campaign season of primaries and state conventions. Of course, it would also be possible for states to preempt any of their existing conventions with a deliberative opinion poll of state voters, should they so choose. Just as primaries proliferated, chiefly in two waves of reform on a state-by-state level, so might these deliberative opinion polls.

Would deliberative opinion polls come out differently from normal opinion polls? Citizens of mass publics show little in the way of knowledge, sophistication, or consistency in their beliefs and opinions. On many issues, about four out of five citizens do not have stable, nonrandom opinions; they have what the political psychologists call "non-attitudes" or "pseudo-opinions." Russell Neuman explains that "most respondents feel obliged to have an opinion, in effect, to help the interviewer out." Even when citizens are "asked if they have thought about an issue enough to have an opinion, 80 to 90 percent of the population selects an alternative in response to most questions. In effect, opinions are invented on the spot."[3]

We do not know to what degree deliberative opinion polls would contribute to thoughtful, self-reflective opinion formation. However, it would seem likely that many of these non-attitudes or pseudo-opinions would be replaced by views that are better rationalized and supported and perhaps more consistent with other elements of the respondents' belief systems.

We can speculate that this kind of event would increase the level of knowledge and sophistication of the voters who participate. Of course, the longer the duration of the event, the more likely would be the effect on the knowledge and sophistication of the participants. Some people have claimed that sophistication correlates with liberalism, others that it correlates with conservatism.[4] Robert Entman argues that "*knowledgeable* nonvoters are significantly more liberal than *ignorant* nonvoters. If ignorant nonvoters became knowledgeable," he speculates, "all else being equal, they might develop new opinions. If they then participated, the beliefs represented at the ballot box might change still more."[5] The same speculation that Entman applies to the possibility of more informed voters throughout the electorate could be applied to our deliberative opinion polls. Entman's conjecture is that the result would be more liberal views.

On the other hand, while knowledgeable nonvoters may be more liberal, knowledgeable voters tend to be more conservative.[6] One might speculate that increasing the knowledge or sophistication of presently less knowledgeable or sophisticated voters might increase their conservatism. Yet sophisticated conservatives are also generally from higher socioeconomic positions. We can only speculate about the ideological results of producing more sophisticated voters from the lower socioeconomic strata.

Neuman argues that "the ratio between liberals and conservatives remains constant across all levels of sophistication."[7] In that case, we need not expect changes in sophistication to affect the ideological distribution, provided that we are affecting sophistication in the same way throughout the sample.[8] Of course, such speculations apply only to the effects of sophistication or knowledge per se. We also have to note that we are creating a situation where people do not merely become more knowledgeable and sophisticated. They interact, face-to-face, with others who are also becoming more knowledgeable and sophisticated. We cannot know, at this point, what changes in the distribution of opinion might result. We are creating an interactive, deliberative, and knowledgeable community that purports to offer a model of what the electorate would come to be if somehow it could be similarly interactive, deliberative, and knowledgeable.

What would it mean for the entire electorate to be so engaged in face-to-face deliberation? As a thought experiment, we might imagine the sample being repeated innumerable times with the same stimulus from candidates until virtually everyone is included. Of course, such a scenario is entirely imaginary and impractical. Nevertheless, it helps us visualize the hypothetical, truly deliberative society of which the deliberative opinion poll is giving us a sample. It is because we can appreciate the moral force of democracy in such a hypothetical, truly deliberative society that we should pay attention to the results of a deliberative opinion poll in our actual society.

The deliberative opinion poll provides a setting in which a representative microcosm of the mass public can become deliberative. Of course, it would be an even greater accomplishment, from the standpoint of democratic theory, if the entire mass public were to become deliberative. But such a result must be considered the province of utopian speculation.

Advocates of direct democracy have sometimes claimed that we only need to bring power to the people for them to become engaged and sufficiently interested in politics to achieve this result of mass deliberation. Robert Paul Wolff, for example, argues that with direct democracy (even in a majoritarian form), "men would learn—what is manifestly not true—that their votes made a difference in the world, an immediate, visible difference. . . . There is nothing which brings on a sense of responsibility so fast as that awareness. America would see an immediate and invigorating rise in interest in politics. It would hardly be necessary to launch expensive and frustrating campaigns to get out the vote. Politics would be on the lips of every man, woman and child, day after day. As interest rose, a demand would be created for more and better sources of news."[9]

This utopian picture is belied by all that we currently know about the effects of our general movement toward direct democracy. Consider, for example, whether referendum issues on the ballot have stimulated citizens to become informed on the issues upon which they will be called to vote. States such as California, Oregon, and Massachusetts have spent millions of dollars on voter's handbooks, which are sent to the residence of every registered voter and which provide detailed information, pro and con, on each issue on the ballot. Depending on the ballot proposition, only from 13 to 33 percent of California voters report making any use of the handbook in response to questions about all of their sources of information.[10] While other evidence shows that those who make use of a voter's handbook are better informed,[11] the problem is to get the public sufficiently engaged to make use of it. In a much earlier study, Joseph La Palombara found that even a sample of college and graduate students could not understand more than about half of the proposals described in an Oregon voter's handbook.[12]

Of course, efforts could be made, and in some cases have been made, to simplify the presentations of information to make them accessible.[13] But the problem of motivation is ever-present. In many ways, it is a classic collective action issue.[14] Wolff argues that with direct democracy people would learn that their votes "make a difference." Collectively they do make a difference, but individually they are minuscule in their impact. Each individual voter has little incentive to become informed on ballot propositions if his or her purpose is to make a difference to the election. In a referendum involving hundreds of thousands or even millions of votes, an individual vote will not perceptibly alter the outcome. The same point can be made about the incentives to vote at all, an issue to which we shall return.

Similar hurdles confront other efforts to increase mass citizen awareness and sophistication with respect to national political issues. There have been serious proposals for a national voter's handbook, a *Citizen's Guide to the 1992 Elections*. There have also been proposals for depositing political information in national computer networks such as Compuserve. In addition, the Center for National Independence in Politics has proposed a test to be made available through newspapers and television that would assist voters in linking up their issue preferences with candidate positions.[15] All of these efforts are useful and laudable. However, it would be utopian to think that they would do much to change the basic level of knowledge and sophistication of the entire electorate. To get nationally representative mass deliberation, a carefully chosen sample under carefully designed conditions seems to be the one realistic possibility.

Several historical and contemporary parallels underlie the deliberative opinion poll. Those worth highlighting are: (a) the use of the lottery in ancient Athenian democracy; (b) the original notion of the American Electoral College; and (c) contemporary experiments such as the *Granada 500* television program in Britain and the Jefferson Center's use of citizens' juries.

The ancient Greek lottery deserves extended discussion. In Athens, it was used to select the Council or Senate; it was used for juries and for most other public officials such as the logistai (a board of thirty who supervised public finances), the archons or magistrates, and such administrative bodies as the supervisors of the public dockyards. The main exceptions were certain roles requiring special expertise, such as military offices and officials of public works. At first glance, this extensive use of the lottery may seem surprising. The first major modern treatise on the subject admits at the beginning: "There is no institution of ancient history which is so difficult of comprehension as that of electing officials by the lot. We have ourselves no experience of the working of such a system; any proposal to introduce it now would appear so ludicrous that it requires some effort for us to believe that it ever did prevail in a civilized community."[16] James Headlam was writing before the rise of modern public opinion polling and the informal adaptations toward what I earlier called the plebiscitary model. It is important to keep in mind, however, the fundamental difference between asking a randomly selected group about their instantaneous and unreflective preferences, as in the case of modern public opinion polling research,[17] and creating a situation where such a randomly chosen group can probe their views on important public issues in depth. The latter alternative is clearly singled out by our proposal for deliberative opinion polls. In certain basic ways, it was also employed by the Athenians.

Of all the ancient Greek institutions that employed the lottery, the one that most closely parallels our proposal is the use of citizens' juries. The juries had much broader range and discretion than do our modern juries, and they would typically number around five hundred.[18] As Headlam notes, "these political trials were really an opportunity for the expression of popular favour or distrust."[19] Every major political leader was charged in the courts, many several times. Aristophon, we are told, was "accused and acquitted 70 times."[20] The trial would not, strictly speaking, be on the stated charges: "The accusation was simply an occasion for an attack. The verdict was not on the accusation, it was on the whole life of the man; it was a vote of confidence or non-confidence given by the people as a result of their observation of his political career, a vote of the same kind as that which in England is given at a general election."[21]

One of the most important uses of these juries was for the *graphe paranomon*—"a court procedure whereby a man could

be tried, convicted and heavily fined for making an 'illegal proposal' in the Assembly." The jurors, so far as modern commentators can determine, had virtually a free hand in determining
what might constitute an illegal proposal. It is especially striking that one could be convicted even if one had succeeded in
persuading the Assembly to accept one's proposal.[22] These court
proceedings thus represented a higher deliberative body than
the Assembly. In contrast to the common assumption in our day
that direct democracy must be superior to representative institutions in expressing the voice of the people,[23] the Athenians,
who possessed the paradigmatic version of direct democracy in
the Assembly, viewed it as subordinate to the political decisions
of a group selected by lot who were empowered (in the graphe
paranomon) to explicitly reconsider and overturn the decisions
of the Assembly.

This court procedure also provided an incentive for speakers
in the Assembly to consider their proposals carefully, because
they might well have to defend them during a second round of
deliberations before a random sample of citizens.[24] The jury
system thus spurred deliberation not only in the jury itself but
also in the Assembly.

It is misleading to think of these institutions as courts in our
modern sense. They were miniature, statistically representative versions of the entire citizenry who were given wide discretion in making political judgments for the polity: "The role of
the juries as the demos in miniature," notes Finley, "implied a
political consciousness and a corresponding, to us, unthinkable,
latitude in arriving at a verdict."[25]

It is a mark of our limited information about ancient Athens
that we have been left no developed defense of their widespread
use of the lottery. Commentators are, however, agreed that its
appropriateness was widely accepted. Socrates' criticism of the
lottery was clearly outside the mainstream of political opinion.
He argued that "it was silly that the rulers of the city should be
appointed by lot when no one would be willing to employ a pilot
or a carpenter or a flautist chosen by lot."[26] The nearest we have
to a defense is a private oration of Demosthenes about a dispute

between half-brothers, one of whom is suing to have the same name as the other. The absurdity of granting this suit is that if the name were then called by lot for a public office, how would it be clear which brother had been appointed? The only recourse would be to go to court, "and we shall be cheated of the fair and equal right, that the one chosen by lot shall hold office. Then we shall berate each other, and he who shall prevail by his words will hold office."[27] It was regarded as unacceptable that the results of the lottery should be frustrated merely by the fact that one person was a better talker than the other. The presumption was clearly that every citizen must have a "fair and equal right" to hold office through the lottery.

The courts were a central democratic institution. Introducing selection by lottery to the Council or Senate was a means of breaking the power of a hereditary Senate so that it could be made subservient to the Assembly.[28] But the Assembly itself was, as we have seen, subservient to the judgments of the courts populated by statistically representative jury panels of five hundred or more. These courts were the ultimate voice of the people in ancient Athens. When pay for jurors was introduced by Pericles, it was a crucial step in bringing power to the people regardless of social class because it permitted all of the social strata to participate in the jury system on an equal footing.[29] Just as we would claim that deliberative opinion polls represent a form of democracy that is preferable to ordinary opinion polls (because they show what the entire electorate would think about an issue under conditions where it would have the time, resources, and opportunity to think about it), so the precedence given to the mass citizens' juries over the decisions of the Assembly shows that the Greeks regarded this opportunity to reconsider the Assembly's actions as representing, in a comparable way, a *higher* form of democracy.

The fate of Socrates shows, however, that the nearly unlimited latitude permitted for these trials provided opportunities not only for deliberation and political equality (among citizens) but also for probable violations of our nontyranny condition.[30] Unless there are constraints on what the people may decide, there will be occasions when they decide, collectively and after much thought, to do bad things. Once more, the quest for institutions that fulfill all three of our conditions—political equality, deliberation, and nontyranny—is a troubled one.

The mere fact that citizens are provided an occasion to think does not guarantee the correctness, either moral or political, of their conclusions. This strategy for better adapting democracy to the large-scale nation-state should not be regarded as a panacea for all political problems. Yet if the opportunity for real deliberation is not sufficient for political and moral correctness, it is surely necessary for a viable form of democracy. Without it, we have mere unreflective preferences open to collective manipulation and pseudo-legitimation. The fact that a deliberative random sample of citizens may, on occasion, be persuaded to do something regrettable does not, in other words, undermine the claim that such a sample can solve our central problem of how to combine deliberation with political equality. It only shows that the decision-making context for such a sample must have constraints that guard against nontyranny (if tyrannous actions are a possibility on the agenda).

Peter Laslett argues that we are haunted by the metaphor of face-to-face democracy inherited from the Greeks. However, when we specify the conditions necessary for face-to-face democracy, they are generally outside the reach of institutions in the large-scale nation-state. "It may be because we have never been able to transcend the face to face assumptions of Greek political thinking that we are unable to develop a political analysis appropriate to our true situation." Laslett asks us to overcome what others have termed our "polis envy."[31] I will suggest that one way of doing so is to invent new institutions that come close to satisfying his seemingly impossible conditions. My claim is that the deliberative opinion poll is an example of that kind of institution.

Laslett sets down four conditions for a "face to face society": that the participants know each other; that important decisions be made by people meeting and talking together; that the society be very small; and that the participants interact. He bor-

rows a biological metaphor, holding that the participants maintain "synaptic contact." They are like parts of a single brain, a
collective mind, which instantaneously interchange electrical
charges. "In a face to face society," he explains, "social synaptic
contact . . . can obviously be made at the maximum ease, speed
and continuity, both ways between each unit and in all directions over the whole mass."[32]

This ideal may have been achieved, at least to some considerable degree, by the Greek polis. While our modern representative institutions sometimes foster such a sub-society among
their elite participants, it is only a media illusion that citizens
could be connected to their leaders in anything remotely reminiscent of such a society in the large-scale nation-state. Yet the
quest for direct democracy, and the quest for representative institutions to move in the southwestern direction in figure 1,
often profit from a similar illusion. Hence, the force of Theodore
Lowi's notion that the media have given us the "Personal Presidency," one that maintains a direct relation to each voter un-
mediated by party or by secondary institutions.[33] When exam-
ined, this illusory quest has depended on an atomistic picture of
isolated citizens: citizens who react to events presented by the
mass media or presented by direct-mail campaigns, and who
react in parallel acts of isolation on election day or by return
post. Such isolated citizens do not have the social bases for
deliberative interaction.

As Jane Mansbridge notes, building on Laslett's notion of the
face-to-face society, "present-day proponents of direct democracy usually assume that this would involve referenda, and do
not even consider the possibility of direct democracy in a face-
to-face context. Neither proponents nor critics of referenda discuss the isolated and anonymous character of decisions made in
a voting booth or how eliminating face-to-face contact among
legislators might affect the relationship among citizens."[34]
Note, of course, that when citizens vote in referendums, they
are in a sense the legislators who have lost face-to-face contact.
They have also lost the social conditions for effective interactive
deliberation.[35]

The case for direct democracy in the large-scale nation-state often ignores the difference between the face-to-face social context of the polis and the modern referendum applied to a mass society. "Proponents of the initiative and referendum," David Magleby notes, "frequently cite as examples of the successful operation of this process the Greek city-states, Swiss cantons, and New England town meetings."[36] But this process is not the same process outside the social context of the face-to-face society.

I believe that twenty-five hundred years of experience show us that deliberative direct democracy must satisfy something very much like the conditions Laslett isolates for the face-to-face society. Participants must know each other well enough to deliberate together. They must meet and discuss issues together. The group cannot be too large to accomplish this task. And they must interact more or less "synaptically." They must interconnect in their discussions. The process of discussion must not be merely one-way. Other conditions having to do with education and some presumption of equality among the participants (at least for purposes of a dialogue of mutual respect) might also be added.

If it is correct that the conditions of the face-to-face society are necessary for *direct* deliberative democracy, then we are faced with the problem that those conditions seem to be inappropriate for the large-scale nation-state. Our dilemma is that face-to-face direct democracy is ruled out by the scale of the nation-state, but that representative democracy seems to be undermined by issues of political equality. Representative institutions, as we have seen, are capable of deliberation, but they are too often corrupted by spillover effects from economic and social inequalities. Hence, we arrive at another version of our initial dilemma: that our choice seems to be between a kind of politically equal but nondeliberative direct democracy (primaries and referendums) and a kind of deliberative but not politically equal representative democracy.

Yet deliberative opinion polls provide the possibility of recreating the conditions of the face-to-face society in a manner that serves democracy in the large-scale nation-state. For while the society served may be large, the face-to-face society in a deliberative opinion poll is itself small. Of course, if the delegates meet for only a few days, the condition that the participants know each other will be satisfied in only a weak sense. In my initial proposal, I specified that the meetings last two weeks. In that more ambitious version,[37] and in others that might be possible, the condition would be more fully satisfied. Nevertheless, even at our proposed National Issues Convention, the participants will deliberate together in an interactive fashion, the group will be small, they will come to know each other, and they will be expected to come to their decisions through mutual discussion and debate. The basic point is that deliberative opinion polls offer direct democracy among a group of politically equal participants who, as a statistical microcosm of the society, represent or stand for the deliberations of the whole. The institution is, in that sense, a direct face-to-face society for its participants and a representative institution for the nation-state.

Returning to the problem of electing the president of the United States, let us recall the connections between the original rationale for the Electoral College and my proposal for deliberative opinion polls. The Electoral College was originally intended to constitute a deliberative body. Of course, the plan to which the Founders eventually agreed has the electors meeting in their respective states rather than all together in a single site. However, it was originally envisaged that the electors would, in fact, deliberate together in a single site, but this plan was abandoned because of the practical difficulty of getting the most capable people to undertake such a journey from the more distant states merely to decide the one issue.[38]

The Founders resisted direct election of the president by the people. George Mason argued that the difficulty with direct election would have been "that an act which ought to be performed by those who know most of Eminent characters & qualifications, should be performed by those who know least."[39] Not anticipating the rise of political parties, the Founders thought of presidential selection in terms of determining the most meritorious individual for highest national office.[40] They struggled to devise a selection system that would accomplish this task but preserve the president's independence from the legislature. At one point, they even gave serious consideration to the use of a lottery that would create a special body drawn from the legislature to deliberate on the most qualified individual. The lottery would have permitted a smaller deliberative body to discern the best-qualified candidate. By the creation of such a separate body, the connection between the legislative and judicial branches would have been made less direct than in a straightforward vote of the legislature. There is speculation that this proposal was influenced by the example of the Athenian lotteries.[41]

At the time, the proposal the delegates finally agreed on was one of the least controversial proposals to emanate from the constitutional convention. As Alexander Hamilton concluded, "If the manner of it be not perfect, it is at least excellent." Hamilton went on to describe a small deliberative body capable of discerning true merit among the candidates: "The immediate election should be made by men most capable of analyzing the qualities adapted to the station and acting under circumstances favorable to deliberation, and to a judicious combination of all the reasons and inducements which were proper to govern their choice. A small number of persons, selected by their fellow citizens from the general mass, will be most likely to possess the information and discernment requisite to so complicated an investigation."[42]

As things have turned out, all deliberative independence has been removed from the electors by the popularly accepted ideology of direct-majoritarianism. As the selection of electors within each state was made more direct by taking it out of the hands of the legislatures, it became more and more difficult for the electors to view themselves as anything other than messengers transmitting the popular vote (either on a district level or, with the unit rule, on a statewide level).[43] As Henry Jones Ford concluded, "Public opinion suppressed the constitutional discretion of the electoral college, and made it a register of the result of the popular vote as taken by states. The President became the elect of the people, the organ of the will of the states."[44]

I am not, of course, arguing that the Electoral College should now be revived as a deliberative body. The haphazardly chosen electors are not representative, and they are not given the occasion for any real deliberation. Furthermore, millions of Americans vote in the expectation that the results will be determined by popular vote totals, either on a state-by-state basis or, implicitly, on a nationally aggregated basis (at least as a normative if not a legal matter). Given these social practices and expectations, departures from the voting totals by individual electors rightly produce moral outrage. "Faithless electors" are breaking their trust with the people. Even the attempts to organize groups of unpledged electors, as with the Dixiecrats of 1948 or the unpledged southern electors of 1960 (who hoped to throw a close election into the House of Representatives),[45] do not play a constructive role. The basic problem is how to combine political equality, deliberation, and nontyranny. Regional bargaining among elites, if an election were thrown into the House, would only steal a popularly determined election. It would not bring about political equality combined with deliberation.[46]

As I have already noted, attempts to combine political equality with deliberation are extraordinarily difficult. Institutions modeled on the deliberative opinion poll resuscitate the Founders' vision of a nationally representative deliberative body playing a role in presidential selection, but in a manner that takes account of the rise of political parties, the development of new technologies of communication, and the continental scale to which our society has grown since their time. A carefully circumscribed, advisory role for such deliberative polls in the process of candidate selection offers a real chance to promote our core values without any danger of seeming undemocratic through some effort to supplant popular elections from making the final decisions.

Some recent efforts in both Britain and the United States have key elements in common with our proposal. The *Granada 500* is a remarkable series on British television that has used a random sample to question national party leaders immediately before elections. In 1974, 1979, 1983, and 1987, Granada Television selected a random sample of about five hundred voters from a benchmark constituency in northern England such as Preston or Bolton (whose voting patterns were taken as a statistically appropriate microcosm of the entire country). One advantage in taking a benchmark constituency rather than a national sample is that it was practical for the voters selected to meet for a two-week period before the program. After studying summaries of the party programs, they questioned experts representing conflicting positions. Some of the experts were academics and some were representatives of the parties. The process culminated in a train ride to London, where the participants questioned the leaders of the three major political parties on national television. Without prepared statements, each leader was subjected to twenty minutes of questioning on the Monday evening before the Thursday general election.

The *Granada 500* differs from my proposal in several obvious ways. First, Granada used a benchmark constituency, not a national sample. Second, the event was meant to influence the general election, not the choice of candidates. Third, no vote or poll of the participants was released before the election. The *Granada 500* was not a "deliberative opinion poll" in the sense proposed here. Rather, the representative sample was employed to create an innovative forum for dialogue with the party leaders on national television.

On at least two occasions, the *Granada 500* was combined with a polling facility, but it was an electronic hook-up of viewers watching the event. This "Electronic 500" provided a poll, not of the face-to-face deliberators, but of ordinary citizens whose unreflective opinions were meant to reflect the viewing public. The Electronic 500 should be viewed as a contribution to the plebiscitary model; the *Granada 500*, by contrast, is a pathbreaking experiment that lays the groundwork for the national telecast of deliberative opinion polls.[47]

A proposal in the same spirit comes from the Jefferson Center for New Democratic Processes in Minnesota. Ned Crosby, president of the center, has proposed "electoral juries" of twelve to eighteen persons who would monitor the United States presidential campaign in various parts of the country, weigh testimony from competing witnesses or experts, and make public recommendations.[48] The Jefferson Center has experimented for a number of years with "policy juries" that have grappled with issues such as the impact of agriculture on water policy and the ethics of organ transplants. The juries of the Jefferson Center have the advantage of interacting in very small groups (typically twelve) that are broadly representative of the population in the same flexible way that a standard twelve-member jury is. The practice of the Jefferson Center has been to have local juries deliberate and then elect representatives to a statewide policy jury that makes final recommendations. While the local juries tend to be loosely representative of the entire population, the representative character of the statewide jury depends on the vagaries of the elections.[49]

Something very much like the Jefferson Center policy juries was proposed by Robert Dahl in *After the Revolution*— statistically representative panels of citizens who could make recommendations on specific policy issues.[50] Dahl has recently gone on to offer the dauntingly ambitious proposal of a "minipopulus" of a thousand citizens who would deliberate on a single policy issue for more than a year. They would be connected "electronically" on an ongoing basis but could otherwise continue their daily lives. Although they would not meet (except through electronic interaction), the extended time proposed for deliberation would clearly mark an advance over any such effort that has yet been tried.[51]

The advantage of electronic interaction is, presumably, that the response rate can be kept high despite the time the participants would have to devote to the project. Most people would hesitate to give up a year of their lives, even to a worthy public purpose. However, if the participation of a national sample can be rendered compatible with other obligations, then the extra time available for deliberation is clearly an asset. Although Dahl does not specify what he means by "electronic" interaction, Amitai Etzioni has worked out concrete and sensible plans for how such an "electronic town hall" might operate. Unlike many of the proposals for "teledemocracy,"[52] Etzioni's work is predicated on the assumption that "a reasoned, informed, broadly shared position requires dialoguing." Until now, "live (real-time) dialogues have been virtually impossible, and communication remains unidirectional. One result of such unidirectional communication is the increasing alienation of the citizen from political and social processes." Without dialogue, even with those who disagree, Etzioni concludes, "the positions that citizens are likely to take tend to be impulsive, uneducated, and unnecessarily polarizing." With this requirement in mind, Etzioni works out a number of specifications for an electronic town hall that he calls "Minerva" (the ancient Greek goddess of political wisdom) for "Multiple Input Network for Evaluating Reactions, Votes and Attitudes."[53] If Minerva were combined with Dahl's notion of a minipopulus, meeting for more than a year and designed to provide the members of the electronic town hall with incentives for participating and paying attention, then a deliberative opinion poll of an even more advanced variety could be achieved.

John Burnheim has proposed the use of representative samples of voters from various affected interests as part of a self-consciously "utopian" scheme to replace all elections with what he calls "demarchy." He suggests that samples representing affected interests in various issue areas be used instead of elected institutions. Affected interests might be determined by opinion poll data or by the judgment of institutional actors. Burnheim's proposals clearly differ from mine, first, because they are utopian, and second, because the notion of what the sample is to represent is quite different. He proposes to represent affected interests, while I propose to represent the entire electorate in what I call a deliberative opinion poll. His proposal is designed to replace elected officials as we know them. My proposal is designed to better select them, to better launch the primary season of presidential selection.[54] The context I have emphasized—candidate selection in the United States—is not utopian. It is a strategically chosen practical arena desperately in need of an alternative model of democracy.

Deliberative opinion polls are not the only possible way of achieving both deliberation and political equality. Since it is possible for familiar representative institutions to muster a great deal of deliberation, reforms directed at curing their faulty realization of political equality would serve these aims as well. It is worth suggesting in this connection a proposal first formulated by Philippe Schmitter and Claus Offe to devise representation vouchers.[55] If the main problem with representative institutions is not their realization of formal equality (because participants have equal voting power as measured by any of the familiar formal indexes), then the problem is primarily the way in which economic inequalities affect the hearing that views may get in the political process. A voucher for representation of interests may greatly improve things in this respect. As opposed to the inequalities fostered by PACs, such a system would democratize the pluralistic system of interest articulation, bringing it within the reach of everyone.

Suppose every citizen could assign a voucher to his or her chosen interest groups. If the amount of the voucher were substantial, say a hundred dollars, it would bring about a massive transformation in the process of interest articulation and representation in this country. If the voucher were much more modest, say five dollars, there would still be a very substantial effect because of the massive numbers of people involved. We might imagine that the voucher could be divided so that organizations could compete for just a portion of one's voucher. The vouchers could only be cashed in, say once a year, by organizations that satisfied some minimum regulatory requirements that ensured, basically, that they were not fraudulent, that they were not-for-profit, and that they acted appropriately to represent the interests they claimed to represent. If every member had a voucher, there would be incentives for organizations to compete with each other to speak for the underclass, the dispossessed, the invisible, the quiescent. Some organizations might well be created just to monitor other organizations. Provided that the barriers to entry in this competition were kept low, there would be a continual dynamism in the creation of organizations and, hence, in the creation of effective voices, where before there had been only silence and indifference. If every citizen had a voucher for representing his or her interests, and if those vouchers could fund interest groups that would compete for the opportunity to competently articulate those interests and lobby on their behalf, the pluralist model would have been successfully reformed in such a way that everyone's interests got a hearing. The central objection to representative institutions on grounds of political inequality would have been set to rest.

Such a proposal would, of course, be enormously expensive. Yet given the hundreds of millions of dollars spent on campaign finance and on PACs, it would be a cheap investment in redressing our grossly unequal process of interest articulation. No matter what innovations are arrived at for selected samples in experiments such as the deliberative opinion poll, there is no escaping the fact that we will have to be governed by representative institutions, not by institutions modeled on the face-to-face society. In that case, we need to think about reforms of those institutions that might achieve both political equality and deliberation. As I have proposed it here, the deliberative opinion poll is a way of affecting candidate selection. But even were such an institution adopted, there would still be the issue just described of interest articulation to elected officials. The voucher is intended to bring political equality to the elected institutions of representative democracy. Both strategies, the voucher and the deliberative opinion poll, are part of the overall effort to achieve political equality and deliberation at the same time.

The representation voucher would be more effective in moving the system toward political equality if the campaigning system's voracious appetite for money could somehow be curbed. As the spectacle of the Keating Five demonstrates, many of the practices which politicians routinely pursue to raise money for elective office come close to selling more than access; those practices, at least as engaged in by some, come close to selling benefits to contributors through legislation. There is a gray area of legislative behavior that raises stark questions about the spillover effects of economic inequalities onto the political process.

Many forms of campaign finance reform might do a great deal to solve this problem.[56] As Max M. Kampelman has proposed, a plausible first step would be to curb the need for such large fundraising efforts by providing free media time to candidates. "Free from the necessity to raise vast sums of money," Kampelman argues, "and accompanied by full disclosure requirements, candidates would be less tempted to engage in fund raising efforts that broach ethical gray areas." Television licenses are granted in the public interest; as Kampelman notes, "for a democracy there is no greater public interest than fair elections and an informed electorate."[57]

A third innovation is also worth discussing. I have in mind Bruce Ackerman's notion of the "constitutional moment."[58] Ackerman's proposal is not an innovation in the same sense as the two just discussed. Unlike a deliberative opinion poll or the organizations created by the representation voucher, it is not a new event, institution, or organization. It is an innovation of a different kind. It is a way of thinking about constitutional events that have already taken place, or that could take place in the future.

Ackerman's argument is relevant to us because the dilemma I have focused on throughout this book—the hard choice between the nondeliberative (formal) political equality of the masses and the deliberative political *in*equality of the elites—is based on the presumption that the masses will not be sufficiently engaged or aroused to be deliberative on national issues in the large-scale nation-state. Ackerman shows that there is one further possibility. The masses may become engaged *episodically*. There may be moments of crisis when everyone is open to continuing, deliberative mass discussion. In these moments of crisis, the masses are aroused and the consensus they arrive at is a voice of the people that can be taken to trump the results of normal politics. Most of the time the people are not aroused. At present, for example, we have low turnouts and mass disaffection. As Walter Dean Burnham has shown, recent (electoral vote) landslide elections of Reagan and Bush are a mandate only in the thinnest sense because they rank among the lowest in American history in terms of the percentage of those eligible to vote who actually ended up voting for the winner.[59]

For Ackerman, most politics most of the time is "normal politics." But there is, on occasion, a "constitutional moment" when the people are aroused and mass collective deliberation is possible. Ackerman's position is that such moments have a higher legitimacy precisely because they represent a kind of collective deliberation that is normally absent. In American history, Ackerman believes there have been three fully developed constitutional moments—the Founding, Reconstruction, and the New Deal. The principles and shared understandings agreed to during those constitutional moments define a basis for judicial review in times of normal politics. They define a basis for constitutional change outside the formal amendment process. As a result, they also provide a solution to the "counter-majoritarian difficulty" that has seemed to afflict judicial review: how can nine old justices of the Supreme Court set aside legislation that was passed in a procedurally fair way to represent the will of the people? Ackerman's solution is that the principles defined by the constitutional moment represent a higher democracy because they arise from the deliberative will of the people at those special moments when the people are aroused.

In that sense, there is a parallel between Ackerman's claims for the notion of a constitutional moment and my claims for the notion of a deliberative opinion poll. The first important difference, however, is that Ackerman is offering an interpretation of our actual Constitution. His claim is that this is the way we should think about our history and the official, legally binding requirements of our actual Constitution. Constitutional moments in his sense are not advisory; they are legally binding

events in the changing structure of our Constitution. By contrast, my notion of a deliberative opinion poll is intended first as
a demonstration, and then as a component of the complex process we call the presidential selection system. It does not trump
or supplant other representative institutions as we know them,
and it does not lay claim to a higher legitimacy. It is merely a
process that would make our system better satisfy all of our
proposed conditions of deliberation, political equality, and nontyranny.

A second difference worth noting is that Ackerman's proposal purports to be a self-sufficient theory of the normative
constraints on constitutional change. Here he faces a theoretical problem that does not apply to either of our proposals (the
deliberative opinion poll and the representation voucher).

Constitutional moments, as he defines them, have no constraints against tyranny of the majority. They have no such constraints precisely because they are the basis for defining the
constraints against tyranny of the majority as those constraints
operate in normal politics.

Suppose that sometime in the future there were a fascist
constitutional moment in the United States. We have only to
imagine a backlash against non-English speakers or illegal al-
iens or some other vulnerable minority. Ackerman's account of
constitutional moments simply specifies the opportunities for
debate and the degree of mass engagement. It is entirely consonant with our hypothetical horror story. Would such a result
then legitimate tyranny of the majority?

Ackerman's position would be, I believe, that such a turn of
events could legitimate tyranny of the majority as a matter of
constitutional law, but not as a matter of normative political
theory. His theory is proposed as the best account of the Constitution we actually have. It is not, however, proposed as an
account of the best possible constitutional system. It would be
entirely compatible with his position to admit that a normatively better system would include constraints against tyranny of the majority. It just happens to be the case that our

present system is not that normatively better system, even though it might be normatively better than most of its competitors.

Each of these innovations has its imperfections. Nevertheless, all three—the deliberative opinion poll, the representation voucher, the constitutional moment—are aimed at the problem of clarifying when the people speak. Each is meant to offer an improvement over the present state of normal politics. Each is meant to better adapt deliberative political equality to the large-scale nation-state. At present, the voice of the people can be distorted by nondeliberation, as when the polls of the plebiscitary model are taken as their voice; or it can be distorted by political inequality, as when our representative processes are distorted by ineffective hearings and spillover effects; or it can be distorted by tyranny of the majority, as it was for generations of slaves when a portion of the population was oppressed and denied the minimal requirements of human decency. Our three essential conditions for a fully adequate democratic system are requirements for the voice of the people being a voice worth listening to. The innovations I have speculated about are meant to show the possibility of a better version of democracy in the large-scale nation-state. By themselves they are not panaceas; they are meant, rather, as a preface to a more adequate democratic practice.

Afterword: The 1992 Campaign and Beyond

The National Issues Convention, announced by the Public Broadcasting Service in July 1991, did not, in the end, take place in the 1992 campaign season because of funding difficulties. However, WETA (the Washington, D.C., public television station) has already joined with all ten of the nation's presidential libraries (five Republican and five Democratic) in efforts to mount such an event for national broadcast in January 1996.

The 1992 nominating process fit the pattern presented here of a process that is neither representative nor deliberative. The sound bites continued to shrink, the invisible primary had a major influence, turnout in the primary process was down and small, self-selected electorates determined the results. While many candidate debates were broadcast, they had very low viewerships during the primary season (unlike the spectacular audience that watched the general election debates).

By contrast, the general election period clearly offered events suggesting movement toward the deliberative poll. Electronic "town meetings" in various formats, viewer call-ins, and the rise of "talk-show democracy" all broke the pattern of earlier campaigns. Instead of staged photo-opportunities and carefully limited access to candidates, citizens were presented with a host of chances to question candidates live on national television, unfiltered by the media professionals. These new forums opened up the process. However, the voices they let in were generally self-selected and off-the-cuff rather than representative and deliberative. Talk-show democracy added a refreshing spontaneity, but its results fell far short of the process proposed here under the heading of "deliberative polls."

To put the new developments in perspective, it is worth distinguishing four types of events:

a) *debates*, where candidates talk to each other as stimulated by questioners or moderators in various formats;

b) *town meetings,* where candidates or office holders talk with eclectic groups of voters;[1]

c) *representative forums,* where candidates talk with random samples of the citizenry; and

d) *deliberative polls,* where candidates talk with random samples of the citizenry who are prepared on the issues and who are then polled about their responses after the deliberative process.

The 1992 season offered numerous examples of debates and town meetings. The second presidential debate at the University of Richmond approached realizing (c), except that the forum employed a sample of undecided voters rather than a sample of the entire electorate. A repeat of the *Granada 500* in the 1992 British general election also showed the viability of representative forums, with the additional dimension that the voters in the *Granada 500* are briefed on the issues so as to add an element of deliberation. The *Granada 500* employed a random sample of five hundred from a benchmark constituency questioning the three party leaders (John Major and his rivals) right before the election. Because the *Granada 500* does not involve any polling of the participants, it is not a deliberative poll. It fits in category (c), representative forums. Category (d), a full-scale deliberative poll, has yet to be tried, although the apparent success of the smaller-scale experiment offered by the Citizens' Jury in the 1992 Pennsylvania Senate race offers suggestive support for the concept. The Citizens' Jury employs too small a sample (typically eighteen or twenty-four) to provide margins of error that would permit a breakdown of the voting to be statistically meaningful. Nevertheless, such experiments continue to suggest how citizen deliberations followed by voting from a full-scale random sample could be employed to advise the public before elections or referendums. Developments from 1992 are, in other words, tantalizingly close to realizing all four of our categories. One hopes that enough momentum has been created to complete the agenda for 1996.

In the afterglow of an American general election that stimulated increased turnout, record viewership of presidential debates and continuing indicators of increased political interest even after the conclusion of the campaign (there were, for example, record numbers of faxes and phone calls from the mass public to both the White House and the Congress during the first days of the Clinton presidency), it is easy to forget that the 1992 nominating process offered a very different picture—a clear continuation of the desultory trends of 1988.

Turnout in the primaries reached an all-time low for the modern era since primaries proliferated after the McGovern-Fraser reforms. In 1992, turnout in the primaries was down 8 percent in comparable states from 1988 levels. Democratic primary turnout came from only about 12 percent of the eligible voting age population; Republican turnout came from only about 8.3 percent. Bill Clinton's important win in the Georgia primary, for example, with 57 percent of the vote, occurred with a turnout of just 18.3 percent in that state; hence, his victory was based on support from only about one eligible voter in ten. Overall, turnout in the southern primaries, which played a crucial role in Clinton's road to the nomination, was down 27 percent from 1988 levels. Turnout was also dispiriting in the Northeast (at least outside New Hampshire, which with 41 percent of the eligible voters achieved the highest turnout of this year's primaries). New York's tabloid primary, for example, attracted participation from only about 7 percent of the eligible voters. Democratic participation in New York was down 39 percent from 1988 levels.

As in previous years, crucial contests turned on tiny, self-selected primary electorates, unrepresentative of their states in the general election and disproportionate in their influence on the process because of their effects on subsequent primaries through the momentum they generated. Even in Maryland, a state with relatively good turnout this time, exit polls showed that 50 percent of the primary voters were at the college-graduate or postgraduate level in education. Blue-collar voters simply did not show up in that primary. The crucial Florida primary was dominated by voters over sixty and by Jewish voters, groups that were both susceptible to Clinton's negative ads about Paul Tsongas on Social Security and on Israel.

As the process approached the climax of Super Tuesday, a *New York Times* poll of "likely primary voters" nationwide reported "no opinion" levels for the then five leading Democratic candidates ranging from 52 to 75 percent. Such a poll reveals an overwhelming pattern of inattention and nonengagement even from the select group of those few citizens deemed "likely" to participate. Furthermore, to the extent that voters acquired an opinion about the contenders, it was likely to be formed from smears published in supermarket tabloids or impressions that a candidate had the image of being substantive without the voters knowing very much about the substance at that stage.

The accident that New Hampshire was in dire straits economically probably conditioned the entire beginning of the 1992 campaign. If Tom Harkin had not run and if relatively prosperous Iowa had started things off, imagine how different the initial debate and the framing of issues would have been. Remember that in 1988 Bush was bounced around by an economically depressed Iowa but restored by what was *then* a prosperous New Hampshire. The arbitrariness of the ordering of these events and the conditions in any one state in a given campaign year strongly reinforce the argument for a nationally representative and deliberative beginning to the process.

As in previous years, the "invisible primary," the period before the first event when candidates jockey for credibility and fundraising, proved crucial. Clinton was generally deemed to be so far ahead before the first event that even a flurry of tabloid allegations just before the New Hampshire primary could not dislodge him. The only actual contest during the preparatory period was the "Florida Straw Poll," an event which Clinton, like Jimmy Carter in 1976, used to his advantage. He took the "poll" more seriously than the other candidates and used his victory to orchestrate both publicity and fundraising. Instead of the "invisible primary" being keyed to events such as the Florida Straw Poll, which, after all, represents party activists in only one state, our proposal would focus the invisible primary around a nationally representative and deliberative event on national television—the National Issues Convention.

Even though poll results shift like sand sculptures in bad weather, they are reported as if they were solid constructions capable of supporting platforms and candidacies. The political landscape was altered beyond recognition when Bush's approval ratings dropped two-thirds, from 91 percent (in the afterglow of the Gulf War) to 30 percent (in his low during the campaign); or when an enigmatic billionaire was able quickly to climb the polls from nowhere to become, if only briefly, the apparent leading candidate for the presidency without having contested a single election. When Gen. Norman Schwartzkopf was substituted for Perot as a presidential challenger in one poll, he did almost as well, revealing the thinness of the public information base on which the Perot challenge was resting.

As contrasted with the talk shows and town meetings, conventional news coverage continued to tightly filter opportunities for the candidates to talk directly with the public. In well-known parallel studies, Kiku Adato and Daniel C. Hallin showed that the average candidate sound bite, the period during which a presidential candidate could speak uninterrupted on the evening news, shrank from about 42 seconds in 1968 to about 9 seconds in 1988. Studies of the 1992 primary season by the Center for Media and Public Affairs show how this shrinkage continued, reducing to an average of 7.3 seconds during the primary season. A similar study for the 1992 general election produced an overall average of 8.4 seconds. In an effort to counteract this trend, CBS announced that it would adhere to a guaranteed minimum length of 30 seconds for candidate sound bites. However, the policy was discontinued after it resulted in a number of candidate statements simply being skipped altogether. The candidates have now apparently learned to speak in 9-second sound bites in order to try to get on the evening news. The transition back to a more extended discourse would depend on the complex interaction of network norms of coverage and candidate calculations. In the meantime, the effective political discourse reaching the mass public continues to be mostly the shrinking sound bite, a medium that reduces political debate to messages worthy of bumper stickers or fortune cookies.

Debates constituted an important effort to provide a more extended dialogue to the public. During the period when there were several active candidates in the primary season, from December 15 to March 15, there were eleven nationally televised debates. While these debates offered a substantive contribution for those who listened, they did not transform the effective political discourse reaching the mass public. By and large, the public was aware of them from the sound bites they produced on the evening news rather than from the experience of watching the debates themselves. Ratings of the major network broadcasts ranged from a low of 2.1 for the climactic CNN/League of Women Voters debate before the New Hampshire primary to a high of 5.5 for the ABC debate March 5 in its "Nightline" slot (each rating point is a percent of the 92.1 million households with television and represents about 921,000 households). These ratings put the debates squarely in the bottom ninth of network programing in their respective weeks. Unlike the final presidential debates of the general elections, primary debates, when candidate selection is a live issue, have not attracted large audiences.

It is worth noting that these debates, when they were turned into sound bites and newspaper stories, were reported mostly in terms of whatever conflict, controversy, or confrontation they happened to generate. The first debate on NBC was most notable for the flap over Jerry Brown's advertising his toll-free telephone number on the air and for Harkin holding up a dollar bill to symbolize the value of the proposed middle-class tax cut. The CNN debate in New Hampshire was reported mostly in terms of the fire Tsongas drew for his support for nuclear power. The Denver debate is remembered for Tsongas's response to Clinton that although he might not be "perfect," at least he is "honest." The Dallas debate was notable for Clinton's rejoinder to Brown that he should "chill out," a phrase for which Hillary Rodham

Clinton later took credit in the press. The WLS Chicago debate the Sunday before the Illinois and Michigan primaries was sparked by Brown's exaggerated description of a *Washington Post* article about alleged conflicts of interest arising from Mrs. Clinton's law firm in Arkansas. Brown described the *Post* as alleging Clinton had "funneled" business to his wife's law firm.

These debates, with the possible exception of the MacNeil/Lehrer debate on PBS, were less than enlightening, even for those few citizens who watched them. Yet the principal difficulty is that to the extent the debates reached the mass public, they did so primarily in terms of sound bites chosen for drama or conflict, sound bites that could be recycled on national and local newscasts. The debates, while a noble effort, did not transform the effective discourse reaching the public.

Another noble effort in 1992 was the opportunity the Discovery Channel provided to all the major candidates to communicate directly to the public. Without the filters of pundits or editors, the candidates could speak to the public directly for twenty minutes each. Unfortunately, the broadcast achieved a rating of only about 1.5, reaching about 1.2 million of the nation's television households. Because the format was not productive of drama or conflict, it was not widely reported and it produced very few sound bites.

A major departure this campaign season was the use of talk shows. Perot, for example, announced his possible candidacy on "Larry King Live" on CNN. Both Clinton and Perot fielded questions from viewer call-ins on the "Today Show" and on "CBS This Morning." Perot held a two-hour "Nightline" town meeting on ABC, whereas Clinton held a ninety-minute town meeting on MTV in his effort to court the youth vote. Clinton used the nationally televised town meeting format nine times during the campaign. (He also used it twice more within his first month in office, demonstrating how the dividing line between campaigning and governing has become more and more blurred.) In one of the most elaborate formats of the campaign, Clinton and Al Gore appeared for two hours on "CBS This Morning" with questions from a studio audience, live satellite connections to

remote locations around the country, and questions collected
from viewer letters. This format was successful in combining
viewer input from around the country with follow-up questions
from the talk-show hosts so as to yield a more sustained dialogue.

President Bush joined in the town meeting format, most notably with hand-picked visitors to the White House on "CBS
This Morning." Bush commented that town meetings were
nothing new. He had, after all, campaigned in 1980 and 1988
with broadcasts of voter forums entitled "Ask George Bush."
However, those forums were scripted, a practice that got Bush in
trouble on the eve of the campaign season when he was heard to
complain to a live mike in December 1991 that he had been
asked the questions in the wrong order in what was supposed to
be a spontaneous teleconference with a California teachers' convention.

Talk-show discussions connecting citizens with candidates
permit us to hear the candidates for longer than a shrinking
sound bite, and they do so under conditions that may produce
spontaneous interchanges. Furthermore, they permit the substantive concerns of ordinary citizens to intrude upon the questions of the press. Instead of press questions focusing on the
horse race and political strategy, ordinary citizens have tended
to raise questions about the economy, health care, and other
issues that touch their lives directly. However, while citizen
questions on the talk shows have been notable for their substance (if not for their follow-ups), host questions have brought
with them a whiff of the sensationalism that is part of the normal agenda of such shows. Talk shows tend to treat politicians
as just another group of celebrities. Hence it was Phil Donohue
who relentlessly pursued Clinton about Gennifer Flowers and
the draft before the New York primary, only to be upbraided by a
member of his studio audience who wanted more substantive
questions. And when Stone Phillips interviewed Bush for
"Dateline NBC," he was reprimanded by an indignant President, who suggested he might cut short the interview rather
than face a question about alleged adultery, a question Phillips

was told he should be "ashamed" for asking in the inner sanc-
tum of the Oval Office.

Some variations of the talk show or town meeting hold out
the promise of even bigger departures from current coverage.
Not only may the viewers get an exposure to lengthier, less
scripted dialogue breaking through the filter of shrinking sound
bites on the evening news, but they may also see their reactions
to what is shown on the screen tabulated, in some process that
appears analogous to voting. This was, of course, the basic idea
behind Perot's proposal for the electronic town hall. As Perot
described it, major issues, such as the national debt or health
insurance, would be explained on the air "in depth, not in sound
bites," and then viewers calling an 800 number would "respond
by Congressional district." This feedback from the people
would be tallied and used to get the White House and Congress
"dancing together like Fred Astaire and Ginger Rogers."

Something very close to Perot's proposal was actually broadcast on the eve of the campaign season in January 1992. CBS
followed the President's State of the Union address with a program called "America on the Line." In a pilot for a possible
series, CBS tabulated about three hundred thousand viewer responses to questions about the President's speech and the state
of the union. However, the viewers who decided to phone in
their responses to the CBS program presented a distorted picture
of public opinion, at least when contrasted with poll results
from a representative sample asked the same questions (and
reported by CBS). For example, 53 percent of "America on the
Line" respondents said they were "worse off" at the time compared to a year ago earlier, while only 32 percent of the representative sample said so. Only 18 percent of "America on the Line"
respondents reported being in basically the "same" economic
situation as a year earlier, while 44 percent of the representative
sample reported being "the same."

This kind of electronic town hall has two fundamental
defects—it is neither representative nor deliberative. It is not
representative because the sample is self-selected. Instead of
being chosen through the methods of modern survey research,

through a random statistical process, viewers at home select themselves by their decisions to call in. The electronic town hall is not deliberative because it demands off-the-cuff responses from viewers at home, who have not had an opportunity for extended face-to-face discussion and reflection.

Viewers calling an 800 number constitute what Norman Bradburn, director of the National Opinion Research Center at the University of Chicago, has called a SLOP—a self-selected listener opinion poll. A SLOP played a role in distorting media coverage of the Carter-Reagan presidential debate in 1980, when ABC used viewer call-ins (in this case with charges for calling a 900 number) to declare Reagan an instant two-to-one winner, as compared to random samples that viewed the debate as a close contest. Like the *Literary Digest* fiasco of 1936, which predicted a landslide for Alf Landon over Franklin Roosevelt, self-selected samples will draw disproportionately from those who feel strongly enough to select themselves. Large numbers do not, by themselves, offer any indication that the viewers who select themselves represent public opinion. CBS has reported that more than twenty-four million calls were attempted to "America on the Line," but far more accurate results could have been achieved from a carefully constructed random sample of several hundred.

The other main problem with this kind of electronic town hall is lack of deliberation. Citizens are expected to phone in their reactions off-the-cuff after listening to a broadcast. They have little opportunity for debate, for consideration of alternative views, and they have little background on factual issues to bring to the discussion. A major problem with direct democracy in the large-scale nation-state is that individual citizens have little reason to invest time and attention in improving the quality of their voting decisions because they can easily calculate that an individual vote is unlikely to have much effect on the outcome.

It is worth noting that one of the more inventive departures this election season has been directed at this information problem. The Center for National Independence in Politics con-

ducted "Project Vote Smart" providing an 800 number, adver-
tised on CNN, which citizens could call to get nonpartisan
information about candidate positions. The same device, advertising a number for citizen information on television, also has
less noble uses. The notorious Floyd Brown (of Willie Horton ad
fame from 1988) attempted to employ this strategy in a new
form of negative campaigning, using a televised ad inviting
viewers to dial in to hear conversations between Clinton and
Flowers.

For better or worse, such new strategies do not affect the
fundamental problem of incentives for individual voters in the
large-scale nation-state to invest time and effort in acquiring
the information that would improve the quality of their votes.
Most citizens are "rationally ignorant," as Anthony Downs put
it in his classic *An Economic Theory of Democracy*. Citizens
can see that their individual votes are unlikely to make any
difference, so why should they go to a lot of trouble evaluating
the candidates and the issues? They may, as a by-product of their
other activities, acquire a gloss of information, but the basis
for choice available to individually rational voters falls far
short of the aspirations of democratic theory.[2] Proliferating primaries, referendums, and opinion polls have brought power directly to the people, but under conditions where the people have
little motivation to think about the power we would have them
exercise.

The premise of the deliberative poll is that a small group, a
statistical microcosm of the whole, can overcome the rational
ignorance of voters in the large-scale nation-state. Each voter in
a televised deliberative poll will have a major part in decision-
making of national consequence. There is every reason to believe such voters will be effectively motivated to take the deliberations seriously. Just as Mancur Olson argued that large
groups face a collective-action problem for the provision of
public goods that small groups do not, the device of the deliberative poll would transfer the problem of incentives for information from a large group (the population at large) to a small group
(a statistically representative microcosm).[3] While there has

been little empirical work on the operation of deliberative microcosms, continuing efforts to hold the *Granada 500* in Britain and Citizens' Juries in the U.S. suggest that serious citizen deliberations with samples that are not self-selected are eminently possible. The subject however, awaits more empirical work.[4]

Perhaps the most dramatic departure this campaign season came in the second presidential debate held at the University of Richmond. A random sample of 209 undecided voters from the Richmond area provided the questions for the candidates. The citizens' questions differed dramatically from those put by journalists in the preceding debate and offered striking evidence that ordinary citizens can successfully direct the substance of the campaign to issues that matter to their daily lives, particularly issues about jobs and the economy.

The Richmond debate was not a SLOP, but neither was it a deliberative poll. The random sample was not prepared on the issues (as has been the practice in the *Granada 500*) and it was not polled afterward about its views. Still, the event shows that with the right incentives, candidates and random samples of voters can be motivated to participate credibly in a televised event timed to have maximum impact on the electoral process.[5] If television is to play a substantive rather than a trivializing role in our campaign process, we can only hope for many more experiments along these lines.

A French television experiment two and a half weeks before the referendum on the Maastricht treaty in September 1992 also showed how ordinary citizens can be brought actively into the televised debate preparing public opinion for a referendum. President François Mitterand answered questions from a panel of fourteen "typical" citizens in the most widely watched event in the referendum campaign. Although the sample was too small to be statistically representative, the three-hour program demonstrated how a discussion with ordinary citizens can enrich the dialogue and better prepare the public for its responsibilities in a referendum.

In the United States the 1992 campaign also stimulated a

legacy of popular input of a different sort, one that suggests distinctions among competing models of democracy. The image of democratic reform to which Americans commonly aspire is one of direct democratic deliberation, reminiscent of the Athenian Assembly or the New England town meeting. But the unprecedented wave of public input through phone calls and faxes in the first days of the Clinton administration focused on hot-button issues fanned by radio talk shows. Phone calls and faxes communicated both numbers and intensities about such issues as attorney general nominee Zoë Baird's childcare arrangements and gays in the military.[6]

The political sensitivity to such waves of intense opinion suggests a different model of democracy—the Shout. Ancient Sparta elected members of the Council by having the candidates appear in random order, stimulating cheers whose volume was judged by impartial judges listening in another room.[7] While Aristotle dismissed this method as "childish,"[8] the volume of shouting has become a proxy for a kind of informal democracy emphasizing intensity. Modern versions of the Shout even sometimes employ electronic measures of intensity such as those used by administration focus groups rating approval levels to President Clinton's first town meeting in Detroit.[9] This practice has spread around the world. The general election debate in Australia, for example, was broadcast in 1993 with instantaneous levels of approval response pictured in a corner of the screen as the debate unfolded. Public viewing of the debate was, in other words, filtered through the aggregate "perceptor meter" rankings of a sample of undecided voters turning dials of approval and disapproval as the debate proceeded.[10]

While technology has long been the key to adapting ancient Greek city-state forms of democracy to the large-scale nation-state, these uses suggest that we are in danger of realizing the Spartan rather than the Athenian model. With luck, perhaps the deliberative poll can be employed to resuscitate yet a third form—not the Shout, and not the Assembly, but rather the Athenian use of the lottery to create a deliberative microcosm.

Notes

1. Toward a New Democracy

1. What would it mean for the entire electorate to be engaged, even hypo-thetically, in face-to-face deliberation? One way to give this image more concreteness is to imagine the sample being replicated over and over many times with each sample being subjected to the same process of debate and face-to-face interaction, until the entire population was covered. Through such a thought experiment we can *imagine* what it would be like for the entire population to have a fully appropriate chance to deliberate about the issues and the candidates.

2. The methodology for delegate selection is essentially the same as that which has been developed for sample surveys. However, for a deliberative poll the delegates must be persuaded to travel to a single site and interact with one another and with the candidates. If the event is dramatized in the media and if all delegates are sufficiently compensated, a reasonable re-sponse rate can be expected.

3. This chapter is based on my "The Case for a National Caucus: Taking Democracy Seriously," *Atlantic,* August 1988, pp. 16–18.

4. My colleague, the statistical expert Mel Hinich, has calculated that if a simple random sample were employed, the margin of error would be plus or minus 4 percent for polls involving the entire sample. If the sample split equally between self-identified Democrats and Republicans, the margin of error for polls of either party would be 5.6 percent.

5. I have served for the past year as the chief academic adviser to this project for WETA.

6. See the discussion of political equality below in chapter 4.

7. In some ways, our deliberative opinion polls can be considered giant focus groups. Focus groups are sometimes employed in political campaigns to provide data on more deeply probed volitions than the often transitory preferences reported in opinion polls. The deliberative opinion poll differs from a conventional focus group in being statistically representative of the entire population. Instead of a focus group of a dozen or so, we propose to employ a national focus group of six hundred or more.

8. Arthur T. Hadley, *The Invisible Primary* (Englewood Cliffs, N.J.: Pren-tice Hall, 1976), pp. 188–95.

9. See Larry Bartels's excellent study *Presidential Primaries and the Dynamics of Public Choice* (Princeton: Princeton University Press, 1988).

10. Ibid., p. 4.

11. See S. Robert Lichter, "Misreading Momentum," *Public Opinion,* May–June 1988, pp. 15–17, 57; the quotation is from p. 16.

12. Scott Keeter and Cliff Zukin, *Uninformed Choice: The Failure of the New Presidential Nominating System* (New York: Praeger, 1983), pp. 118–21.

13. Gary R. Orren and Nelson W. Polsby, "New Hampshire: Springboard of Nomination Politics," in Orren and Polsby, eds., *Media and Momentum: The New Hampshire Primary and Nomination Politics* (Chatham, N.J.: Chatham House, 1987), pp. 1–8; quotations on p. 6.

14. "Mondale Urges Primary Plan," *New York Times,* June 9, 1988, p. B10.

15. See Thomas Cronin and Robert Loevy, "The Case for a National Pre-primary Convention Plan," *Public Opinion* 5, no. 6 (December–January 1983), pp. 50–55.

16. Everett Carl Ladd, "A Better Way to Pick Our Presidents," *Fortune,* May 5, 1980, pp. 132–35, 139, 142.

2. Size and Democracy

1. See Robert A. Dahl and Edward R. Tufte, *Size and Democracy* (Stanford: Stanford University Press, 1973), esp. chap. 1, for a useful overview of this problem.

2. *The 'Politics' of Aristotle,* Ernest Barker, ed. and trans. (New York: Oxford University Press, 1958), 1326b, pp. 291–92. See also Peter Laslett, "The Face to Face Society," in Laslett, ed., *Philosophy, Politics and Society* (Oxford: Basil Blackwell, 1956), pp. 157–84. See p. 177 for the point about Aristotle and divine order. Laslett also notes that the ideal society in Plato's *Laws* had to maintain a constant number of no more than 5,040 citizens (p. 163). See also my discussion below of the democratic character of Athenian juries chosen by lot.

3. For eighteenth-century Americans, the term *democracy* usually indicated a small, direct democracy. They struggled to find the right terminology for their experiment with large-scale representative democracy. As Gordon Wood notes of Americans in the 1780s, "Their governments were so new and so distinctive that they groped for political terms adequate to describe them. By the late 1780s Americans generally were calling their governments democracies, but peculiar kinds of democracies." They were "democratic republics" or "representative democracies." See Wood, *The Creation of the American Republic: 1776–1787* (New York: Norton, 1972), p. 595.

4. Clinton Rossiter, ed., *The Federalist Papers* (New York: New American Library, 1961), p. 104. Hereafter cited as *Federalist.*

5. Ibid.

6. Patrick Henry's speech of June 9, 1788, at the Virginia Ratifying Convention as quoted in Douglas Adair, "That Politics May Be Reduced to a

Science: David Hume, James Madison and the Tenth Federalist," *Huntington Library Quarterly* 10 (1956–57), pp. 343–60; quote on p. 348.

7. Adair, "That Politics," p. 348.

8. See Baron de Montesquieu, *The Spirit of the Laws*, translated by Thomas Nugent, with an introduction by Franz Neumann (New York: Hafner, 1966), book 8, chap. 16, p. 120.

9. Ibid., book 2, chap. 2, p. 9.

10. Hume had in mind a scheme of indirect elections where 10,000 parishes would each elect one representative; these representatives would be grouped in groups of 100 on a countywide basis who would elect "senators." See David Hume, *Essays and Treatises on Several Subjects*, vol. 2 (Edinburgh, 1793), pp. 514–15. For the connection between Hume and Madison, see Adair, "That Politics." See also the discussion in David Epstein, *The Political Theory of 'The Federalist'* (Chicago: University of Chicago Press, 1984), esp. pp. 101–02.

11. For an attempt to systematize this argument, see Robert Dahl, *A Preface to Democratic Theory* (Chicago: University of Chicago Press, 1956), esp. pp. 11–19. For a critique of Dahl's interpretation of *Federalist* no. 10, see Robert J. Morgan, "Madison's Theory of Representation in the Tenth Federalist," *The Journal of Politics* 36 (1974), pp. 852–85.

12. *Federalist* no. 45, p. 349. For further discussion of Madison's commitment to political equality, see Morgan, "Madison's Theory," esp. pp. 863–64, and Cass Sunstein, "Beyond the Republican Revival," *Yale Law Journal* 97 (1988), pp. 1,539–90, esp. n. 75, p. 1,553.

13. *Federalist*, p. 73.

14. See Montesquieu, *The Spirit of the Laws*, book 9, chaps. 1–3, pp. 126–28.

15. Cecelia M. Kenyon, ed., *The Antifederalists* (Indianapolis: Bobbs-Merrill, 1966), Introduction, p. xxxix.

16. Herbert J. Storing, *What the Anti-Federalists Were For* (Chicago: University of Chicago Press, 1981), p. 17.

17. Yet we sometimes delude ourselves that the face-to-face character has been retained. See Laslett, "The Face to Face Society" for an excellent discussion of how the face-to-face metaphor has been transplanted, misleadingly, to the modern nation-state. For a description of the development of small-scale, face-to-face democracy in an American town, see Charles S. Grant, *Democracy in the Connecticut Frontier Town of Kent* (New York: Columbia University Press, 1961). Grant shows how face-to-face democracy tended to become ever more inclusive. Legal restrictions about who could supposedly participate in town meetings were increasingly ignored as it was difficult not to let everyone in the room participate (pp. 128–33).

18. Giovanni Sartori, "Video Power," *Government and Opposition*,

Winter 1989, pp. 39–53, esp. p. 48. By "poll direction," Sartori means a process parallel to David Riesman's famous notion of "other direction."

19. For experimental work on how strongly television viewers are influenced by newscasts in their judgment of the importance of issues, see Shanto Iyengar and Donald Kinder, *News That Matters* (Chicago: University of Chicago Press, 1987).

20. Michael Oreskes, "America's Politics Loses Its Way as Its Vision Changes World," *New York Times*, March 18, 1990, pp. 1, 22.

21. Robert A. Dahl, "The Pseudodemocratization of the American Presidency," lectures delivered at Harvard University, April 11 and 12, 1988; published in S. McMurrin, ed., *The Tanner Lectures on Human Values* (Cambridge: Cambridge University Press and University of Utah Press, 1989), pp. 35–71; quotation on p. 67.

3. The Lure of Direct Democracy

1. For a balanced overview of what is now a large literature, see F. Christopher Arterton, *Teledemocracy: Can Technology Protect Democracy?* (Newberry Park, Calif.: Sage, 1987). For a proselytizing view with reports on one effort to implement the theory, see Ted Becker, "Teledemocracy: Bringing Power Back to the People," *Futurist*, December 1981, pp. 6–9. For a critique of "ersatz participation," see Jean Bethke Elshtain, "Democracy and the QUBE Tube," *Nation*, Aug. 7–14, 1982, pp. 108–10.

2. See Francis X. Clines, "The Shevardnadze Warning: Not Just Content but Timing," *New York Times*, Dec. 21, 1990, pp. A1, A6.

3. Not only specialist Soviet journals but such weeklies as the mass-circulation *Argumenty i fakty* and the smaller-circulation *Moscow News* have published opinion polls on the standing of Soviet politicians, including Gorbachev. I am indebted to Archie Brown for his help on this and related matters.

4. As we will see later, even these efforts to achieve political equality often fall short of anything more than purely formal equality because of inequalities of resources.

4. Three Democratic Conditions

1. I mean by this a familiarity with the essential routines of citizenship and a capacity to process information offered to the general public in debate on public issues.

2. See, for example, John F. Banzhaf III, "Multi-Member Electoral Districts—Do They Violate the "One Man, One Vote" Principle?" *Yale Law Journal* 75 (July 1966), pp. 1,309–38, esp. pp. 1,314–18.

3. We are applying formal political equality here to voters. Complex legal and moral issues arise in determining whether various nonvoters, such as children, criminals, and transient populations, should be counted

in electoral districts. See Paul Brest and Sanford Levinson, "Discussion: The Problem of the Denominator," in *Processes of Constitutional Decisionmaking*, 3d ed. (Boston: Little, Brown, forthcoming).

4. *Federalist*, p. 349.

5. Ibid.

6. Robert J. Morgan, "Madison's Theory of Representation in the Tenth Federalist," *Journal of Politics* 36 (1974), p. 863.

7. I am also assuming that the decision making constrained by the three conditions of political equality has what Robert Dahl has called "final control of the agenda." See his "Procedural Democracy," in Peter Laslett and James Fishkin, eds., *Philosophy, Politics, and Society*, vol. 5 (New Haven: Yale University Press, 1979), pp. 105–07.

8. See, for example, Daniel H. Lowenstein, "Campaign Spending and Ballot Propositions: Recent Experience, Public Choice Theory, and the First Amendment," *UCLA Law Review* 29 (1982), pp. 505–641. See also Larry J. Sabato, *PAC Power: Inside the World of Political Action Committees* (New York: Norton, 1984).

9. James Fishkin, *Tyranny and Legitimacy: A Critique of Political Theories* (Baltimore: Johns Hopkins University Press, 1979), part 1.

10. Fishkin, *Tyranny and Legitimacy*.

11. *Federalist*, p. 82.

12. *Federalist*, p. 432.

13. Dahl, "Procedural Democracy," pp. 104–05.

14. A good summary with some criticisms can be found in Raymond Geuss, *The Idea of a Critical Theory* (Cambridge: Cambridge University Press, 1981), chap. 3. See also Jurgen Habermas, "A Reply to My Critics," in John B. Thompson and David Held, eds., *Habermas: Critical Debates* (Cambridge, Mass.: MIT Press, 1982), pp. 219–83.

15. David Braybrooke, "Changes of Rules, Issue-Circumscription and Issue Processing" (forthcoming).

16. Mill writing in the *Examiner*, July 4, 1832; as quoted in J. H. Burns, "J. S. Mill and Democracy, 1829–61," part 1, *Political Studies* 5, no. 2 (1957), pp. 158–75; quotation on p. 160.

17. "Considerations on Representative Government," in John Stuart Mill, *Three Essays*, edited with an introduction by Richard Wollheim (Oxford: Oxford University Press, 1975), p. 284.

18. Ibid., p. 285.

19. John C. Calhoun, *A Disquisition on Government* (New York: Liberal Arts Press, 1953), p. 30.

20. For a more detailed account, see Clyde Wilson, "Calhoun and Community," *Chronicles of Culture*, July 1985, pp. 17–20: "The minority veto was not a device to block decision but an effort to provoke further deliberation and a higher consensus. It trusted in the consent of the governed, that

is, on the people, to find the right answers, provided the action of a mere majority, which might be a temporary manifestation of selfish combinations, could be suspended long enough to bring into play the higher consensus of communities" (p. 20). My thanks to Clyde Wilson, editor of the Calhoun papers, for stimulating discussions.

21. Calhoun, *Disquisition*, pp. 30–31.

22. For a penetrating discussion of the limitations of the unanimity rule, with applications to Calhoun, see Douglas Rae, "The Limits of Consensual Decision," *American Political Science Review* 69, no. 4 (December 1975), pp. 1,270–94.

23. For a good overview, see John Hart Ely, *Democracy and Distrust: A Theory of Judicial Review* (Cambridge: Harvard University Press, 1980), chaps. 4–6.

24. See Bruce Ackerman, "Beyond Carolene Products," *Harvard Law Review* 98, no. 4 (February 1985), pp. 713–46.

25. See Cass R. Sunstein, "Beyond the Republican Revival," *Yale Law Journal* 97, no. 8 (July 1988), pp. 1,539–90, esp. pp. 1,549 and 1,579, for a discussion of how one purpose of judicial review is to promote deliberation among political officials.

5. The Forms of Democracy

1. The most elaborate contemporary discussion of the values at stake in the northeast quadrant can be found in Giovanni Sartori, *The Theory of Democracy Revisited* (Chatham, N.J.: Chatham House, 1987). For a thoughtful defense of the southwest quadrant in my diagram, see Benjamin Barber, *Strong Democracy: Participatory Politics for a New Age* (Berkeley: University of California Press, 1984).

2. *Federalist*, p. 82.

3. Ibid.

4. For a rigorous variation on the same argument, see Robert Dahl, *A Preface to Democratic Theory* (Chicago: University of Chicago Press, 1956).

5. J. Skelley Wright, "Money and the Pollution of Politics: Is the First Amendment an Obstacle to Political Equality?" *Columbia Law Review* 82 (May 1982), pp. 609–45; quotation on p. 609.

6. See David Mayhew, *Congress: The Electoral Connection* (New Haven: Yale University Press, 1974); Gary Jacobson, "Running Scared: Elections and Congressional Politics in the Eighties," in Mathew McCubbins and Terry Sullivan, eds., *Congress: Structure and Policy* (Cambridge: Cambridge University Press, 1987); Raymond A. Bauer, Ithiel de Sola Pool, and Lewis Anthony Dexter, *American Business and Public Policy* (New York: Atherton, 1968).

7. Randall Rothenberg, "P.R. Firms Head for Capitol Hill," *New York Times*, Jan. 4, 1991, pp. C1, C6. For the earlier background to this development, see Stanley Kelley, Jr., *Professional Public Relations and Political Power* (Baltimore: Johns Hopkins University Press, 1956).

8. Jeffrey K. Tulis, *The Rhetorical Presidency* (Princeton: Princeton University Press, 1987), p. 39.

9. Ibid., p. 96.

10. Ibid., p. 125. The original quotation is from Woodrow Wilson, *Leaders of Men*, ed. T. H. Vail Motter (Princeton: Princeton University Press, 1952), p. 39.

11. For more on Johnson's reliance on polling, see Larry Sabato, *The Rise of Political Consultants: New Ways of Winning Elections* (New York: Basic Books, 1981), n. 7, p. 105. For a detailed account, see Michael J. Towle, "Understanding America: Lyndon Johnson's Interpretation of American Public Opinion, 1963–1968" (paper prepared for delivery at the 1990 Southwestern Social Sciences Association meetings, Fort Worth, March 1990).

12. "Patrick H. Caddell had the closest relationship with an incumbent president of any pollster in history." Sabato, *Rise of Political Consultants*, p. 70.

13. James Baker responded to congressional challenges by citing a "70% approval rating on . . . foreign policy." This statement was widely criticized in the foreign policy community as a departure from past norms. See Thomas L. Friedman, "Baker's World," *New York Times*, Sept. 21, 1990, p. 1.

14. Erwin Knoll, editor of the *Progressive*, on the *MacNeil-Lehrer Newshour*, Nov. 26, 1990. For similar interactions between poll results and presidential behavior, especially in the Reagan and Nixon administrations, see Samuel Kernell, *Going Public: New Strategies of Presidential Leadership* (Washington, D.C.: Congressional Quarterly, 1986), pp. 83–84 and chap. 6.

15. Sidney Blumenthal, *The Permanent Campaign* (New York: Simon and Schuster, 1982).

16. Kernell, *Going Public*, p. 138.

17. Blumenthal, *Permanent Campaign*, pp. 10–11.

18. Kernell, *Going Public*, p. 138.

19. Robin Toner, "A Year in Sound Bites: 10 Seconds to Remember," *New York Times*, Dec. 31, 1990, p. 9.

20. *Washington Post*, July 16, 1979; quoted in Tulis, *Rhetorical Presidency*, p. 3.

21. Tulis, *Rhetorical Presidency*, pp. 5–6.

22. Theodore J. Lowi, *The Personal President: Power Invested, Promise Unfulfilled* (Ithaca: Cornell University Press, 1985), chaps. 5 and 6.

23. James Ceaser, *Presidential Selection: Theory and Development* (Princeton: Princeton University Press, 1979), pp. 5–6.

24. Lowi, *Personal President,* p. 20.

25. Robert Paul Wolff, *In Defense of Anarchism* (New York: Harper and Row, 1970).

26. See *Tyranny and Legitimacy,* chap. 8.

27. *Federalist,* p. 384.

28. Charles W. Anderson, *Statecraft: An Introduction to Political Choice and Judgment* (New York: Wiley, 1977), pp. 208–09.

29. *Federalist,* p. 385.

30. Carole Pateman, *Participation and Democratic Theory* (Cambridge: Cambridge University Press, 1970), p. 42. See chaps. 3–5 for a discussion of workplace democracy.

6. The March toward Direct Democracy

1. Alexis de Tocqueville, *Democracy in America,* trans. Henry Reeve (New York: George Adland, 1839), p. 4.

2. For a general account, see Alan Grimes, *Democracy and the American Constitution* (Lexington, Mass.: Lexington Books, 1978).

3. Walter Dean Burnham, *The Current Crisis in American Politics* (New York: Oxford University Press, 1982), p. 82.

4. Walter Dean Burnham, "Why Americans Don't Vote" (forthcoming). Burnham calculates a notional turnout rate for 1880. Even if one made the wild assumption of a 10 percent undercount in the census, the notional turnout would fall to only 79 percent, he concludes. Claims about high historical turnouts in the U.S. resist skeptical probing, although some allowances for election fraud should probably be included.

5. David Glass, Peveril Squire, and Raymond Wolfinger, "Voter Turnout: An International Comparison," *Public Opinion,* December–January 1984, pp. 49–55; quotation on p. 52.

6. Glass, Squire, and Wolfinger note that two trips are required for same-day registration in some states (Maine and Oregon, whose turnout rates were 64.6 and 61.5 percent, respectively, in 1980). But this explanation does not apply to Wisconsin or Minnesota, whose higher turnout rates we used for this supposition. The other factor they emphasize—exclusion of some ballots in the United States (spoiled ballots and those who vote, but not for president)—could only explain slight differences (see ibid., p. 53).

7. Ibid., p. 50.

8. Arthur T. Hadley, *The Empty Polling Booth* (Englewood Cliffs, N.J.: Prentice Hall, 1978), esp. chap. 3; quotations on pp. 68, 74; see also table 3, p. 154.

9. Raymond E. Wolfinger and Steven J. Rosenstone, *Who Votes?* (New Haven: Yale University Press, 1980), pp. 108–09.

10. Robert Pear, "Number of Ballot Initiatives Is the Greatest since 1932," *New York Times,* Nov. 5, 1990, p. A11.

11. Arnold Hamilton, "The Vanishing Electorate: Why People Don't Vote," *Dallas Morning News*, Nov. 1, 1990, p. 7H.

12. The proliferation of referendums has of course taken place only on the state level. Arendt Lijphart shows that the United States "is one of only four of the long-term democracies—the others are Israel, Japan, and the Netherlands—in which a national referendum has never been held." Cited in Robert A. Dahl, "The Pseudodemocratization of the American Presidency," in S. McMurrin, ed., *The Tanner Lectures on Human Values* (Cambridge: Cambridge University Press and the University of Utah Press, 1989), p. 59. By contrast, a 1976 study reported that the Swiss had held 124 national referendums since World War II. See Philip Goodhart, *Full-Hearted Consent* (London: Davis-Poynter, 1976), p. 203. Arnold Hamilton, "The Vanishing Electorate: Why People Don't Vote," *Dallas Morning News*, Nov. 1, 1990, p. 7H.

13. David O. Sears and Jack Citrin, *Tax Revolt: Something for Nothing in California* (Cambridge: Harvard University Press, 1982), pp. 222–23.

14. See Thomas E. Cronin, "Term Limits—A Symptom, Not a Cure," *New York Times*, Dec. 23, 1990, p. E11.

15. The Commission on Party Structure and Delegate Selection, *Mandate for Reform* (Washington, D.C.: Democratic National Committee, 1970). See esp. p. 10 for participation and popular control and p. 14 for more democracy being the cure for the ills of democracy.

16. Nelson Polsby, "The News Media as an Alternative to Party in the Presidential Selection Process," in Robert Goldwin, ed., *Political Parties in the Eighties* (Washington, D.C.: American Enterprise Institute for Public Policy, 1980), pp. 50–66, esp. p. 59.

17. Jeanne Kirkpatrick, *Dismantling the Parties* (Washington, D.C.: American Enterprise Institute, 1978), p. 6.

18. See Theodore J. Lowi, *The Personal President: Power Invested, Promise Unfulfilled* (Ithaca: Cornell University Press, 1985), p. 110–12. Strictly speaking, we can consider the increasingly mechanical character of convention decision making (at least with respect to the nomination) as a parallel to the movement noted earlier with respect to the Electoral College. In both cases, since the form of representation has been retained, they can be considered movements south in figure 1.

19. These transformations are usefully described in Kirkpatrick, *Dismantling the Parties*, pp. 13–15.

20. Nelson Polsby, *The Consequences of Party Reform* (New York: Oxford University Press, 1983), p. 73.

21. Harold W. Stanley and Richard G. Niemi, *Vital Statistics of American Politics*, 2d ed. (Washington, D.C.: Congressional Quarterly, 1990), p. 134.

22. See Allen Fraser Lovejoy, *La Follette and the Establishment of the*

Direct Primary in Wisconsin, 1890–1904 (New Haven: Yale University Press, 1941), p. 8.

23. Kiku Adato, "The Incredible Shrinking Sound Bite" (Cambridge, Mass.: Joan Shorenstein Barone Center of the John F. Kennedy School of Government, Research Paper no. 2, June 1990), p. 4. For a view skeptical that the shrinking sound bite really makes a difference, see Martin Plissner, "Inkbites," *Washington Post*, March 20, 1989, p. A11.

24. Reported by Paul Taylor of the *Washington Post* and quoted in *The Voter's Channel: A Feasibility Study* (New York: Alvin H. Perlmutter, Inc., for the John and Mary Markle Foundation, June 1990), p. 28.

25. "Dialogue on Film: Bill Moyers," *American Film Magazine*, June 1990, pp. 17–20, 44, esp. p. 20.

26. Bruce Buchanan, "Electing a President" (manuscript), p. 10.

27. Michael Robinson and Margaret Sheehan, *Over the Wire and on TV* (New York: Russell Sage Foundation, 1983), p. 149. I am grateful to Larry Bartels for bringing these findings to my attention.

28. Robert Luskin, "Measuring Political Sophistication," *American Journal of Political Science* (November 1977), pp. 856–99; quotation on p. 888 (citing Robert S. Erikson, Norman R. Luttbeg, and Kent L. Tedin).

29. Ibid., p. 889. While European respondents would surely do better on the NATO question, Luskin's general point is that the level of sophistication of the American mass public is not unusual in cross-national comparison.

7. Politico-Economic Systems

1. In what sense, for example, did East Germany "return" to democracy? Its people achieved democracy while the state in question ceased to exist. For a useful overview of recent changes, see "New Democracies: The Year the Votes Poured In," *Economist*, Dec. 22, 1990, pp. 43–44.

2. For a related diagram that inspired this one, see C. E. Lindblom's important book *Politics and Markets: The World's Politico-Economic Systems* (New York: Basic Books, 1977), p. 161. The nonmarket alternatives on the economic side of the diagram include what Lindblom would call coercion or hierarchy and what he would call the indoctrination of preceptoral systems, such as that used by the Chinese during the Cultural Revolution. In other words, the nonmarket box collapses together systems that can be distinguished further because of their reliance on either coercion or persuasion in different mixes. As Lindblom emphasizes, there are elements of exchange, coercion, and persuasion in all economic systems. Hence, all of these classifications are a matter of emphasis.

3. For an argument along these lines, see Lindblom, *Politics and Markets*, pp. 162–64.

4. Archie Brown, "Gorbachev's Leadership: Another View," *Soviet Economy* 6, no. 2 (1990), pp. 141–54, esp. p. 142.

5. Jonathan Steele, "Gorbachev Attacked on All Sides," *International Guardian*, Dec. 20, 1990, p. 1. For the view that Gorbachev's evaluation of the necessity of moving to a market economy is closer to Yeltsin's than this quotation might suggest, see Brown, "Gorbachev's Leadership," p. 149.

6. Eduard Bernstein, *Evolutionary Socialism* (New York: Schocken, 1961).

7. See, e.g., Michael Harrington, *Socialism* (New York: Bantam Books, 1970), pp. 42–46, 62–63. Harrington argued that "the secret of the unknown Marx is that he was too optimistic about, too trusting in, democracy" (p. 90).

8. Juan Linz, "Transitions to Democracy," *Washington Quarterly*, Summer 1990, pp. 143–64, esp. p. 157.

9. Adam Przeworski and John Sprague, *Paper Stones: A History of Electoral Socialism* (Chicago: University of Chicago Press, 1986), p. 59.

10. Ibid., pp. 184–85.

11. I am indebted to Claus Offe for suggesting this point to me. A recent heading in the *Economist* dramatized the danger: "Mikhail Sergeevich Pinochet?" As the article concluded: "If Mr. Gorbachev chooses the smack of firm government . . . it might, just might, be the Soviet Union's turn for what could be called the Pinochet approach to liberal economics." See "Order, Order," *Economist*, Dec. 22, 1990, pp. 12–13. After Shevardnadze's resignation, the possibility of a Pinochet model for the introduction of the market was welcomed by some Soviet legislators. See Bill Keller, "Moscow Gossips about Dictatorship," *New York Times*, Dec. 22, 1990, p. 6.

12. There is, of course, some history of military intervention in Eastern Europe as well. However, it is not a history of regular intervention on the Latin American model.

13. Guillermo O'Donnell, *Modernization and Bureaucratic-Authoritarianism: Studies in South American Politics* (Berkeley: Institute of International Studies, 1973). I am indebted to P. Nikiforos Diamandouros of the Greek Institute for International and Strategic Studies for his advice on this section.

14. See Steven Greenhouse, "Czechs Begin to Shift to a Free Market," *New York Times*, Jan. 1, 1991, p. 3.

15. Ibid.

16. See Steven Greenberg, "Year of Economic Tumult Looms for Eastern Europe," *New York Times*, Dec. 31, 1990, pp. 1, 24.

17. Serge Schmemann, "What If There's No Happy Ending in Moscow?" *New York Times*, Dec. 30, 1990, p. E3.

18. For a skeptical account, see Alfred Stepan, "Paths toward Re-

democratization," in Guillermo O'Donnell, Philippe C. Schmitter, and Laurence Whitehead, eds., *Transitions from Authoritarian Rule: Comparative Perspectives* (Baltimore: Johns Hopkins University Press, 1986), pp. 64–84, esp. pp. 83–84. Stepan, however, forcefully describes the "theoretical space" within which such a possibility might be successful under some circumstances (p. 84).

19. Linz, "Transitions to Democracy," p. 160.

20. Remarks of President Zhelyv Zhelev of Bulgaria, conference at the Center for the Study of Democracy, Dec. 17–19, 1990 (proceedings forthcoming).

21. Gorbachev has similarly asserted that the law passed by the Russian republic legalizing private ownership be reversed until a public referendum can be conducted. In the continuing crisis of legitimacy in the Soviet Union, Gorbachev has repeatedly invoked the possibility of referendums as the higher voice of democratic authority. For the referendum possibility, see Bill Keller, "Russia Cuts Share of Soviet Budget by More Than 90%," *New York Times*, Dec. 28, 1990, pp. A1, A4. A referendum served a similar function in Britain's decision to join the Common Market. See Philip Goodhart, *Full-Hearted Consent* (London: Davis-Poynter, 1976).

22. James Miller's penetrating study *Democracy Is in the Streets: From Port Huron to the Siege of Chicago* (New York: Simon and Schuster, 1987) captures the mood: "By exploring its vision of participatory democracy, a generation discovered (and eventually became addicted to) what one young radical called 'breakaway experiences'—political and cultural moments when boundaries melted away and it seemed as if anything could happen. Such moments did, in fact, occur. They arose in the thick of passionate debate, during sit-ins, in marches, at violent confrontations—at times when people, discovering discontents and ideas and desires in common, sensed, often for the first time and sometimes in the teeth of danger, that together they could change the world" (p. 317).

23. See the remarks of Prof. Ivailo Znepolski of Sofia University at the Center for the Study of Democracy, Sofia, Bulgaria, Dec. 17–19, 1990. He rationalized the street demonstrations against the Socialist (formerly Communist) government as a form of "direct democracy."

24. Remarks of Juan Linz at the Center for the Study of Democracy, Sofia, Bulgaria, Dec. 17–19, 1990.

25. See Brenda Fowler, "Slovenes to Vote on Independence," *New York Times*, Dec. 22, 1990, p. 8.

26. The Slovene plebiscite offered an overwhelming expression of popular support for independence: about 95 percent, with a turnout of about 90 percent. See Brenda Fowler, "Slovenes Vote for Autonomy by an Overwhelming Margin," *New York Times*, Dec. 24, 1990, p. 6. Once the people

are given an opportunity to speak unequivocally, options other than the one they endorse will appear undemocratic.

27. The mutual influence between Slovenia and Croatia is an obvious example.

28. Similar forecasts have been made for the Soviet Union. For example, William Hyland has predicted, within five years, a Soviet Union consisting only of the three Slavic republics of Russia, the Ukraine, and Byelorussia (*David Brinkley's Washington*, ABC broadcast of Dec. 23, 1990).

29. See Robert Dahl, "Procedural Democracy," in Peter Laslett and James Fishkin, eds., *Philosophy, Politics, and Society*, vol. 5 (New Haven: Yale University Press, 1979), pp. 97–133, esp. section on "inclusion," pp. 120–29. See also Allen Buchanan, *Secession: The Morality of Political Divorce from Fort Sumter to Lithuania and Quebec* (Boulder, Colo.: Westview Press, forthcoming).

30. See Brian Barry, "Is Democracy Special?" in Laslett and Fishkin, *Philosophy, Politics, and Society*.

31. Ed A. Hewitt, "The Soviet Economic Plan," *Foreign Affairs*, Winter 1990–91, pp. 146–67; quotations on p. 166.

32. See Lee C. Bucheit, *The Legitimacy of Self-Determination* (New Haven: Yale University Press, 1978).

33. Guillermo O'Donnell and Philippe C. Schmitter, *Transitions from Authoritarian Rule: Tentative Conclusions about Uncertain Democracies* (Baltimore: Johns Hopkins University Press, 1986), p. 5; the chess analogy is on p. 66.

8. New Structures of Representation

1. See, however, the discussion of "constitutional moments" below for a vulnerability to tyranny that is, at least, theoretical.

2. The Commission on Party Structure and Delegate Selection, *Mandate for Reform* (Washington, D.C.: Democratic National Committee, 1970), p. 12.

3. W. Russell Neuman, *The Paradox of Mass Politics* (Cambridge: Harvard University Press, 1986), p. 23. See also Philip Converse, "The Nature of Belief Systems in Mass Publics," in David E. Apter, ed., *Ideology and Discontent* (New York: Free Press, 1964), where the notion of a nonattitude was coined.

4. For a good review, see Neuman, *Paradox of Mass Politics*, pp. 73–91.

5. Robert Entman, *Democracy without Citizens: Media and the Decline of American Politics* (New York: Oxford University Press, 1989), p. 27.

6. See ibid. p. 171, n. 42.

7. Neuman, *Paradox of Mass Politics*, p. 78. However, for some cautions about Neuman's model of sophistication and a proposed alternative, see

Robert Luskin, "Explaining Political Sophistication," *Political Behavior* (forthcoming).

8. If the lower socioeconomic strata experience a disproportionate change in sophistication, then there might well be some effect on the eventual ideological distribution of the sample. All of these possible effects are, however, highly speculative.

9. Robert Paul Wolff, *In Defense of Anarchism*, pp. 36–37.

10. David Magleby, *Direct Legislation: Voting on Ballot Propositions in the United States* (Baltimore: Johns Hopkins University Press, 1984), p. 136.

11. Ibid., p. 137.

12. Joseph LaPalombara, *The Initiative and Referendum in Oregon, 1938–1948* (Corvallis: Oregon State College Press, 1950), pp. 119–20. See also the discussion in Magleby, *Direct Legislation*, pp. 137–39, which replicates LaPalombara's basic findings.

13. See Betty H. Zisk, *Money, Media and the Grass Roots: State Ballot Initiatives and the Electoral Process* (Newberry Park, Calif.: Sage, 1987), pp. 62–63. Zisk is pessimistic about the results of simplification because of the intrinsic difficulty of the issues on the ballot.

14. The classic account of the problem is Mancur Olson, *The Logic of Collective Action* (New York: Shocken Books, 1968). For an update and reformulation, see Russell Hardin, *Collective Action* (Baltimore: Johns Hopkins University Press, 1982).

15. These proposals are usefully summarized in *The Voter's Channel: A Feasibility Study* (New York: Alvin H. Perlmutter, Inc., for the John and Mary Markle Foundation, June 1990), pp. 88, 109. For some other creative proposals along these same lines, see Benjamin Barber, *Strong Democracy: Participatory Politics for a New Age* (Berkeley: University of California Press, 1984), chap. 10.

16. James Wycliffe Headlam, *Election by Lot at Athens*, 2d ed. (Cambridge: Cambridge University Press, 1933), p. 1. For a description of the lottery's application to the Council, see chap. 2; for its application to juries, see pp. 35–40; for its application to the logistai, see p. 135; for its application to the archons, see p. 148; for its application to the dockyards, see p. 155; for military exceptions, see p. 102; for builders of public works, see p. 106.

17. Hence the problem of "non-attitudes" or "pseudo-opinions." See Neuman, *Paradox of Mass Politics*, pp. 23–35.

18. M. I. Finley notes that they were not perfectly random by modern standards, as the panel from which they were selected may have overrepresented city dwellers and the poor (who needed the per diem payment). Nevertheless, he concludes, it is "understandable that the Athenians viewed large juries chosen by lot from six thousand of a total citizen popula-

tion of thirty-five or forty thousand as sufficiently representative to count as the demos itself in action." Finley, *Democracy: Ancient and Modern* (New Brunswick, N.J.: Rutgers University Press, 1973), p. 118. R. K. Sinclair terms the juries a "random sample" and points out that the panel of 6,000 was itself determined by lot from the population of those with full citizen rights. Sinclair also points out that orators treated the juries as a cross-section of the citizenry. See Sinclair, *Democracy and Participation in Athens* (Cambridge: Cambridge University Press, 1988), pp. 19–20, 70–71.

19. Headlam, *Election*, p. 36.

20. Ibid., p. 35.

21. Ibid., p. 37.

22. Finley, *Democracy*, pp. 113–14.

23. The classic statement of this position can, of course, be found in Rousseau's *Social Contract* (e.g., book 3, chap. 15). For modern statements of the same position, see Robert Paul Wolff, *In Defense of Anarchism* (New York: Harper and Row, 1970), pp. 32–34, and Barber, *Strong Democracy*.

24. Ibid., p. 114.

25. Ibid., p. 118.

26. Plato *Protagoras* 319b–323a. See the discussion of this passage in A. H. M. Jones, *Athenian Democracy* (Oxford: Basil Blackwell, 1957), pp. 46–48.

27. Demosthenes, *Private Orations XXVII–XL*, trans. A. T. Murray (Cambridge: Harvard University Press, 1918), pp. 455–57. I would like to thank Paul Woodruff for his advice on this passage. See also Jones, *Athenian Democracy*, pp. 47–48.

28. Headlam, *Election*, pp. 46–47.

29. See Josiah Ober, *Mass and Elite in Democratic Athens* (Princeton: Princeton University Press, 1989), pp. 81–82.

30. For a stimulating reconstruction of the events, accompanied by the missing case for the prosecution and speculations on how it could have turned out otherwise, see I. F. Stone, *The Trial of Socrates* (Boston: Little, Brown, 1988).

31. I am indebted to Bruce Ackerman for suggesting this phrase to me in another context, when he challenged me to overcome the same malady.

32. Peter Laslett, "The Face to Face Society," in Peter Laslett, ed., *Philosophy, Politics and Society* (Oxford: Basil Blackwell, 1956), pp. 157–71.

33. Theodore J. Lowi, *The Personal President: Power Invested, Promise Unfulfilled* (Ithaca: Cornell University Press, 1985), p. 20.

34. Jane J. Mansbridge, *Beyond Adversary Democracy* (New York: Basic Books, 1980), p. 275.

35. A success story in achieving Laslett's conditions for face-to-face interaction can be found in the National Issues Forums organized by the Kettering Foundation for volunteer groups of citizens to deliberate on the

issues. For an overview, see "Citizens and Policymakers in Community Forums: Observations from the National Issues Forums" (Dayton: The Harwood Group for the Kettering Foundation, June 1990).

36. Magleby, *Direct Legislation*, p. 3.

37. See my "The Case for a National Caucus: Taking Democracy Seriously," *Atlantic*, August 1988. See also the discussion of Dahl's "minipopulus" below.

38. See Schlomo Slonim, "The Electoral College at Philadelphia: The Evolution of an Ad Hoc Congress for the Selection of a President," *Journal of American History* 73 (June 1986), pp. 35–59. William Houston's argument against the electors meeting together is discussed on p. 44.

39. The small states had another reason for resisting popular election of the president: it would cancel the numerical advantage they had won in the construction of the Congress. This advantage was reproduced precisely by the Electoral College, which at the same time accomplished the goal of removing the choice from control of the Congress. See Slonim, "Electoral College." For the point about the small states, see p. 56. For the quotation from Mason, see p. 47. However, the introduction of the unit rule has, in fact, given the large states an advantage. Banzhaf calculates that "citizens of States like New York and California have over two and one half times as much chance to affect the election of the President as residents of some of the smaller States and more than three times as much chance as citizens of the District of Columbia." See John F. Banzhaf III, "One Man, 3.312 Votes: A Mathematical Analysis of the Electoral College," *Villanova Law Review* 13 (1968), pp. 304–32, esp. p. 325.

40. See James W. Ceaser, *Presidential Selection: Theory and Development* (Princeton: Princeton University Press, 1979), chap. 1.

41. See Richard M. Gummere, *The American Colonial Mind and the Classical Tradition* (Cambridge: Harvard University Press, 1963), p. 45. See also Slonim "Electoral College," p. 45.

42. *Federalist* no. 68, p. 411.

43. Judith Best, *The Case against Direct Election of the President: A Defense of the Electoral College* (Ithaca: Cornell University Press, 1971), pp. 16–18.

44. Henry Jones Ford, *The Rise and Growth of American Politics* (New York: Macmillan, 1898), pp. 213–14.

45. Best, *Case against Direct Election*, pp. 39–40, 166–90.

46. And if the civil rights of some Americans were bargained away, our nontyranny condition would also be violated.

47. The *Granada 500* experience through 1983 is described in Gus MacDonald, "Election 500," in Ivor Crewe and Martin Harrop, eds., *Political Communications: The General Election Campaign of 1983* (Cambridge: Cambridge University Press, 1986), pp. 125–34. My information on events since comes from conversations with Rod Caird, head of factual programs,

Granada Television. I am indebted to him for supplying me with tapes and various documents.

48. "Electoral Juries to Rejuvenate Presidential Politics" (Minneapolis: The Jefferson Center for New Democratic Processes, 1988). I am indebted to Ned Crosby for his helpful discussions about the projects of the center.

49. "Final Report: Policy Jury on School-Based Clinics" (Minneapolis: The Jefferson Center for New Democratic Processes, 1988). See pp. 22–23 for a discussion of these representation issues. See p. 18 for the history of electoral juries at the Jefferson Center.

50. Robert A. Dahl, *After the Revolution: Authority in a Good Society* (New Haven: Yale University Press, 1970), pp. 149–50.

51. Robert A. Dahl, *Democracy and Its Critics* (New Haven: Yale University Press, 1989), p. 340.

52. See, e.g., Ted Becker, "Teledemocracy: Bringing Power Back to the People," *Futurist*, December 1981, pp. 6–9.

53. Amitai Etzioni, "Minerva: An Electronic Town Hall," *Policy Sciences* 3 (1972), pp. 457–74; quotations on pp. 458, 459.

54. John Burnheim, *Is Democracy Possible?* (Berkeley: University of California Press, 1985), esp. pp. 111–13.

55. This voucher proposal is the product of a working group at the Center for Advanced Study in the Behavioral Sciences at Stanford during 1987–88, in which I participated with Claus Offe and Philippe Schmitter. They have their own distinctive versions of this proposal.

56. A thoughtful proposal directed at the system of campaign finance itself is developed by Daniel Hays Lowenstein in "On Campaign Finance Reform: The Root of All Evil Is Deeply Rooted," *Hofstra Law Review* 18 (Fall 1989), pp. 301–68.

57. Max M. Kampelman, "Cut Campaign Costs, Not Spending," *New York Times*, Dec. 20, 1989, p. 27.

58. I take this account from Bruce Ackerman, "The Storrs Lectures: Discovering the Constitution," *Yale Law Journal* 93 (1984), pp. 1,013–72; from his "Constitutional Law/Constitutional Politics," *Yale Law Journal* 99 (December 1989), pp. 453–57; from the manuscript version of his *We the People* (Cambridge: Harvard University Press, forthcoming); and from conversations with Ackerman about his theory of the Constitution and its implications.

59. Ranking presidential elections from 1828 to 1988 in terms of the share of the potential electorate gained by the actual winner, Reagan's election in 1980 stood 37th out of 41 cases and Bush's in 1988 stood 35th. If cases in which a single third party garnered at least 5 percent of the votes cast are excluded, the number of elections drops to 32, with Bush in 1988 ranking 30th. I am indebted to Walter Dean Burnham for sharing these results with me.

Afterword

1. I distinguish town meetings from "electronic town halls" in Ross Perot's sense. The latter are discussed separately below. As self-selected listener opinion polls tabulating the immediate responses of viewers at home, they are neither representative nor deliberative.

2. A useful and creative discussion of this problem can be found in Samuel Popkin's *The Reasoning Voter: Communication and Persuasion in Presidential Campaigns* (Chicago: University of Chicago Press, 1991). Popkin's argument that voters exhibit low information rationality does not stand in the way of my argument that there would be benefits in the "high information" rationality of the deliberative poll. Indeed, a televised deliberative poll would be a prime producer of "cues" by which viewers can assess their interests without investing a lot of additional time and effort.

3. Mancur Olson, Jr., *The Logic of Collective Action: Public Goods and the Theory of Groups* (New York: Schocken, 1971).

4. I am engaged with Shanto Iyengar and Robert Luskin in one such effort, resulting from citizen deliberations with materials prepared for the National Issues Forums.

5. The Richmond debate may have been the most watched program in American television history, with about 62 percent of the nation's households tuning in at some time during the broadcast, according to some estimates.

6. For a good overview, see Kevin Merida and Helen Dewar, "The People Find Their Voice: Washington Is Bombarded with Phone Calls and Faxes," *Washington Post National Weekly Edition*, Feb. 8–14, 1993, p. 6.

7. I have benefited here from the excellent discussion in Jon Elster, *Solomonic Judgements: Studies in the Limitations of Rationality* (Cambridge: Cambridge University Press, 1989), pp. 85–86. See also E. S. Stavely, *Greek and Roman Voting and Elections* (London: Thames and Hudson, 1972), pp. 73–74.

8. Aristotle, *Politics* 1271a9.

9. See *Newsweek*, Feb. 22, 1993, p. 19, for the administration's use of a "dial group" to evaluate the intensity of public reactions to the president's statements in the Detroit town meeting broadcast.

10. See Errol Simper, "The Electronic Campaign: No Frills ABC Beaten by Swingers at Nine," *Australian*, Feb. 15, 1993, p. 6.

Index

Italic numerals indicate notes containing significant information.

Democracy: size of, 14–19, 92–93, 106n2; "pure," 16; direct vs. representative, 42; Madisonian vs. majoritarian, 42, 49; deliberative vs. nondeliberative, 43; representative/Madisonian, 43–45; representative/majoritarian, 45–49; Tocqueville on, 54; and economics, 72–75; and electorate boundaries, 78; Greek, 86–91; and Founders' terminology, 14, 106n3; Hume on, 107n10; and sixties movements, 116n22. See also Democratic transitions; Democratic values; Direct democracy; Direct-majoritarianism; Face-to-face democracy; Plebiscitary model: Representative democracy
Democracy: Ancient and Modern (Finley), 119n
Democracy and Distrust (Ely), 110n
Democracy and Its Critics (Dahl), 121n
Democracy and Participation in Athens (Sinclair), 119n
Democracy and the American Constitution (Grimes), 112n
Democracy in America (Tocqueville), 112n
Democracy in the Connecticut Frontier Town of Kent (Grant), 107n
Democracy Is in the Streets (Miller), 116n22
Democracy without Citizens (Entman), 117n
Democratic party, 60–62, 82
Democratic transitions, 67–68; and direct-majoritarianism, 67, 75–77; and economics, 67–79, 115n11; and Spain, 77; and ethnic conflicts, 77–78; and seces-

sion, 78–79; and decomposition of state, 78–79, 114n1; unpredictability, 79–80
Democratic values, 104; and Mill, 38–40; and Calhoun, 39–40; systemwide vs. individual institutions, 40–41; and participation, 52, 53; and deliberative opinion polls, 95; and Electoral College, 95. See also Deliberation; Equality, political; Tyranny
Demonstrations, 77, 116nn22, 23
Demosthenes, 88, 119n
Denmark, 55
Dexter, Lewis Anthony, 45, 110n
"Dialogue on Film: Bill Moyers," 114n
Direct democracy: vs. republic, 16–17; and Qube system, 21–23; and plebiscitary model, 22–25; and Mill, 38; unanimous, 49–50; and democratic values, 49–53, 59–60, 85; scale, 50–52; and referendums, 59; and demonstrations, 77, 116n23; and voter knowledge, 85–86; and face-to-face society, 91–92; and conventions, 113n18; and Electoral College, 113n18. See also Direct-majoritarianism
Direct Legislation (Magleby), 118n, 119n
Direct mail, 61, 62
Direct-majoritarianism: inadequacy of, 18–20, 24–25; and Qube system, 21; and presidency, 46–49; and voter turnout, 54–55; and democratic values, 64, 67; and democratic transitions, 67, 75–77; and Electoral College, 94–95. See also Direct democracy
Dismantling the Parties (Kirkpatrick), 113n

Geuss, Raymond, 109n
Glass, David, 55, 56, 112n
Going Public (Kernell), 111n
Goodhart, Philip, 113n, 116n
Gorbachev, Mikhail, 70, 79; and
    opinion polls, 24, 108n3; and ref-
    erendums, 67, 76, 116n21
Gore, Albert, 10
Granada 500, 86, 95–96
Granada Television, 95–96
Grant, Charles S., 107n
Graphe paranomon, 87–88
Gray, Robert K., 46
Great Britain, 55, 56, 78, 86,
    116n21; *Granada 500*, 95–96
Greece (ancient), 86–91
Greece (modern), 68–70
Greenberg, Steven, 115n
Greenhouse, Steven, 115n
Grimes, Alan, 112
Gummere, Richard M., 120n

Habermas, Jurgen, 36, 109n
Hadley, Arthur, 56, 105n, 112n
Hamilton, Alexander, 15; on scale
    of democracy, 17–18; on de-
    liberation, 35–36; and Electoral
    College, 94
Hamilton, Arnold, 113n
Handbooks, voter's, 85–86
Hardin, Russell, 118n
Harrington, Michael, 115n7
Headlam, James, 87, 118n, 119n
Henry, Patrick, 15, 106–07n
Hewitt, Ed, 79, 117n
Hill and Knowlton, 46
Hinich, Mel, 105n
House of Representatives, U.S., 95
Houston, William, 120n
Hume, David, 16, 107n
Humphrey, Hubert, 3
Hungary, 68, 73
Hyland, William, 117n28

Idea of a Critical Theory, The
    (Geuss), 109n
"Idea of a Perfect Commonwealth"
    (Hume), 16
Ideology, and political knowledge,
    83–84, 118n8
"Incredible Shrinking Sound Bite,
    The" (Adato), 114n
In Defense of Anarchism (Wolff),
    112n, 118n, 119n
*Initiative and Referendum in Ore-
    gon, The* (LaPalombara), 118n
Interest groups, 45; and "de-
    marchy," 98; and representative
    vouchers, 99–100
Invisible Primary, The (Hadley),
    105n8
Iowa, 2–10
Ireland, 78
Is Democracy Possible? (Burn-
    heim), 121n
Israel, 113n12
Italy, 55, 56
Iyengar, Shanto, 108n

Jackson, Jesse, 5
Jacobson, Gary, 45, 110n
Japan, 56, 113n12
Jefferson Center for New Demo-
    cratic Processes, 86, 96–97,
    121n
Johnson, Lyndon B., 47
Jones, H. M., 119n
Juan Carlos, king of Spain, 70
Judiciary, 41
Judicial review, 102
Juries: citizens', 86; Greek, 87–89;
    electoral, 96–97; policy, 97

Kampelman, Max M., 101, 121n
Keating Five, 100
Keeter, Scott, 6, 106n
Keller, Bill, 115n, 116n